Essentials of Elementary Library Management

Laurie Noble Thelen

Linworth
PUBLISHING, INC

Library of Congress Cataloging-in-Publication Data

Thelen, Laurie Noble.
  Essentials of elementary library management / by Laurie Noble
Thelen.
       p. cm.
Includes bibliographical references.
  ISBN 1-58683-076-7
  1. School libraries--United States--Administration. I. Title.
  Z675.S3T46 2003
  025.1'978--dc21

                              2003012889

Published by Linworth Publishing, Inc.
480 East Wilson Bridge Road, Suite L
Worthington, Ohio 43085

Copyright © 2003 by Linworth Publishing, Inc.

ISBN: 1-58683-076-7

5 4 3 2 1

Table of Contents

Table of Figures

Introduction

There I was, sitting in the doctor's office waiting for my name to be called and thinking to myself how overwhelmed I was—again—with handling new situations and changes at work. I felt like a drowning rat, paddling madly to keep its head above water. Once more, I had inflicted big changes on my life. I was the new librarian in a new district at an established school. "Change is normal, change is good," I kept repeating to myself as if it were my mantra. The worst part was that in spite of my 10 years' experience and graduate school training, I still felt unprepared for these changes, changes that had more to do with the day-to-day life in the library media center trenches. "There should be a book about all the little things that librarians encounter," I mused. And that was the beginning of this book.

It has been said that the best path to learning something is to teach it. I suppose this is true, as it forces you to consider each question from another's point of view in preparing the presentation. Writing this book has been that and more because it has given additional purpose to each frustration I encounter. Now, I reason that if I am having difficulties, I must have a ripe subject about which to pass on lessons learned to other library media specialists.

My years in library services have been more diverse than I would have imagined for one who treasures stability in life. But then, you do not go into education for a static work life, do you? I have worked in a fledgling school that required me to build and move the library three times to different locations in the building. At one point, I did much with "books on casters," working the hallways. Another school presented extra challenges because English was the second language. I have worked in both private and public schools and have seen how different districts respond to their educational missions. I have had the assistance of a media clerk at times, but also the experience of working alone. The positions have offered me the gamut of tools from low tech to high tech. I have opened a new library in a brand new school, been the new kid on the block in an established enterprise, and been labeled the "experienced" library media specialist. I have tried to recall many of the struggles of coping with these changes and challenges along the way for inclusion in this book so that it will be as practical as possible. Whether you are just beginning your librarianship or you have been juggling all of your responsibilities for years, you should find information in these pages that you can use today.

Each chapter is created with the practitioner in mind. Chapter 1 focuses on the creation of a new library and contains collection development advice and guidelines. Chapter 2 reveals how to thrive as an experienced or novice library media specialist in a new district. Time management tips are revealed in Chapter 3 to help you quickly take care of the minutiae and move on to the joy of your profession. Chapters 4 and 5 speak to your administrative role and your day-to-day life in the media center with a sample spreadsheet and tips to conquer grant writing. In Chapter 6, motivational reading programs are provided with sample reading record forms and helpful Web sites. Chapter 7 gives ideas to support the reading advocate role of the library media specialist and collaboration efforts with the classroom teacher. Chapter 8 includes information on how to motivate teachers to make media technology a part of their classroom experiences. Chapter 9 lists strategies to enable you to promote positive student behavior in the library media center. Chapter 10 includes ideas on how to find and keep volunteers and media clerks, and how to create a comfortable workplace. The appendix contains useful forms and addresses to quickly use on the job.

The library media specialist's job is a big one, and this handbook is a companion to take with you on the journey. You are not alone (if you ever felt so), and you have a rare opportunity to touch many lives in a meaningful way.

You will find that *library* and *library media center* have been used interchangeably in this book, as well as the terms *librarian* and *library media specialist*. While typical library management books do not include activities and project ideas, I have chosen to include some of these items to help beginning library media specialists.

It has been said that knowing the *why* of a task provides the motivation for finding the *how* to do it well. In this spirit, and trusting that you remember why, this book of hows is for you, my esteemed reader. May it be a provision to prosper you in your endeavors.

Chapter 1

Planning a New Library Media Center

The quick burst of the camera's bright flash has faded as district notables turn over the dark soil. A new school has been born. Many months and years of preparation have culminated in this one, quick moment. Many more months of preparation continue before the hundreds of students and their teachers discover their new school and its resources. The school's blueprints already present the key areas and features of the library media center, which have been purposefully planned and created. The library media specialist may be hired for the new school project at any point along its development. For this chapter, however, let us assume that the library media specialist has been invited to participate in the process from the beginning. Even if much of the early planning decisions have been made by the time the library media specialist joins the building project, he or she can help create the best library media center by participating in the process.

Participation in Building Committee Plans

Background Research

What goes into creating a great library media center facility? An excellent place to begin is by visiting other schools. Interviews with resident library media specialists should produce a healthy list of preferred design features: aspects that work well and those that the library media specialists would like to see changed if given the opportunity. During this background research time, check out the annual facility design showcase issue of *American Libraries* that is devoted to featuring new and remodeled library spaces. The American Library Association (ALA) publishes *American Libraries Magazine* monthly, except bimonthly in June and July, for its members. Local libraries can subscribe for an annual fee. Read also *Facilities Planning for School Library Media and Technology Centers*, by Steven M. Baule, published by Linworth Publishing, Inc. Build a list of features to try and features to avoid from these and other sources. Draw a sketch of the library, and place the shelves, tables, circulation desk, and other furniture to acquire a feel for the design possibilities. While serving on the building planning committee, review the plans often, and be assertive with ideas—the building will be around for a long time.

Make sure the library media center design and floor plan follow the guidelines of the Americans with Disabilities Act (ADA) of 1990, Title III (revised on July 1, 1994), Part 36, Section 8. The architect will design the library space according to these specifications, but check any furniture arrangements added. The United States Department of Justice publishes ADA Standards for Accessible Design <http://www.usdoj.gov/crt/ada/index.htm>. Work closely with the ADA or adaptive technology consultants to ensure the library media center's compliance.

The new school population may be large or small, or for a restricted age level, such as a fifth grade center. With that said, let us proceed as if a "typical" school of 500–600 children, grades K through 5, is the target plan.

School Floor Plan: Library Media Center Checklist

Check the initial location of the media center in the overall school floor plan. Is the space accessible to all classes, or is it located at one end of the building? The library media center should be an asset and augmentation for every classroom, and the architecture should support this concept. Is the library media center located near a noisy area, such as a main hallway or the cafeteria? While this is not ideal, the solution may be a compromise to meet the goal of accessibility. What will be the traffic patterns in this new school? Answering this question will help illustrate what to expect once the school is operational.

The Library Media Center Space

Main Floor Space: Interior Design

How big should the library be? According to the Texas Administrative Code for School Facilities Planning, the elementary school library should have a minimum of 3.0 square feet times the planned student population, or a minimum space of 1,400 square feet, whichever is larger. The information and standards can be found at <http://www.tea.state.tx.us/technology/libraries/lib_standards_facilities.html>. Request a space large enough to accommodate two full classes of students in the open, or activity, areas. With an eye to the far, or not-so-far, future, remember that schools often accommodate larger student populations with outbuilding additions, but the library media center is not so easily expanded.

The architect will make sure the lighting meets the city code, but you can use your library visits and background research to question the lighting design utility. Request as much light as possible. Consider the problem of glare. If the design includes large windows, plan on adjustable window coverings to block the light during audiovisual presentations. Likewise, some degree of adjustable electric lighting will let you control proper lighting levels and glare by zone. The architect can advise and discuss the subjective effects of different lighting technologies. The most energy-efficient lighting will not necessarily serve the library media center's mission to be a comfortable and accessible resource area. Ask for plenty of electrical outlets throughout the library. Individual temperature control for the media center rooms helps create a comfortable environment for patrons.

Opinions vary about color choices for a library media center. Generally, strong contrasts between floor color and wall color work well. Avoid "busy" patterns in the carpet and the wall. Beige and pastels invoke a calm atmosphere. An interior designer can provide advice for a color palette. If the building planning team does not already involve an interior designer, some designers charge hourly to provide a limited design service.

Shelving Plan

The shelves will hold the permanent collection of the library media center for access by its patrons. How many shelves and what shelf depths are needed? The fiction and nonfiction bookshelf height should be at the 5-foot level with a shelf depth of 10 inches. These shelves hold 8 to 10 books per linear foot, or 30 books per shelf. The picture book shelves should be 42 inches high with a shelf depth of 12 inches. This converts to 15 books per linear foot, or 60 books per shelf. Consideration of possible student growth beyond the immediate plans might dictate provision for about 20% more shelf space for future use.

Activity Areas

Plan for a variety of areas—quiet spaces as well as areas for small and large group instruction. Create a lounge area with magazine shelving and comfortable furniture. Set up a table with a chess game, a puzzle, or a microscope.

Supervision

The ability to give the librarian line-of-sight supervision of the main floor is very important in library media center planning. Are all areas of the library media center visible from the circulation desk? Examine the traffic flow in the floor plan—is it easy to navigate, or does it present obstacles for patrons? The media center should have only one entrance and exit (fire codes may dictate additional emergency exits). Too many exits results in potential losses of materials. Stay away from a two-story or pit-designed space; these make it difficult to supervise students or shelve materials.

Ample phone jacks means that phone messages will be heard promptly. Ask the architect to place one in the office, the workroom, and on the circulation desk. An outside line on each of these phones is a necessity for effective multitasking.

Auxiliary Space

The Workroom

Plan for 250 to 300 square feet for a workroom area. The workroom should have a sink, cabinets, and a bathroom. The bathroom is often overlooked, but not having one greatly affects the time in which the library media specialist is absent from the center. Subsequently, this cost-effective productivity feature (or the lack thereof) will affect scheduling and personnel staffing flexibility. It is worth pressing for in the design phase and nearly impossible to add later.

Cabinets should have locks so that items can be safely stored. Long counter-tops are a necessity in the workroom. Repair and processing of materials takes space. The workroom area needs a window large enough to view activity in the library. Shelves are required to store incoming and outgoing processed materials. Purchase file cabinets to store equipment manuals and other materials. Install a telephone jack and electrical outlets.

The Storage Room

The storage room is a multipurpose room or area of the workroom used to store audiovisual equipment and materials. Ideally, the area should be at least 500 square feet. Security devices, such as locks, should be installed to prevent theft. Electrical outlets are needed for checking the operation of equipment. Shelving should be 15–18 inches deep with the ability to adjust height. In every storage area, pay attention to the distance between the top shelf and the ceiling. Materials should not be placed too high for a person of average height to manage without ladders or additional personnel. Cabinets with drawers are necessary for storing items with small pieces, such as science or math materials and manipulative objects. Flat drawer storage is required for maps, posters, and charts. Remember to allow space for drawer and door openings.

Other Spaces

Conference Room/Area

Small group discussions and audiovisual productions require a separate space. The conference area should be 150 square feet with a window for supervision. A computer drop, electrical outlets on each wall, and a projection screen are necessary. Provisions should be made for either a ceiling-mount LCD projector (preferred) or a tabletop projector and the appropriate power and control wiring in either case.

Professional Reading Room/Area

Find space for teachers to browse books and magazines related to their grade level or expertise. Furnish the area with a couch, magazine rack, and shelving. When the time comes for stocking this area, enlist suggestions for materials from the staff, and ask other library media specialists about materials to include in the professional collection. Make this space accessible. Do not place the professional collection in a closet or on a shelf behind the circulation desk. Instead, find an area on the library floor, and purchase a comfortable chair. As an added benefit to planning the professional space, opportunities should arise for the library media specialist and classroom teachers to discuss and plan collaborative activities.

Closed-Circuit Television Broadcast Room/Area

The TV studio can be a part of the workroom, a conference room, or part of the storage room. Students or faculty broadcast daily and special announcements. Equipment needed for low-cost broadcast operation includes a videocassette recorder, a camcorder, a sound mixer, and microphones. You also need to purchase cables to connect the camera and microphones to the VCR and sound mixer. Lapel microphones work well for student anchors who are seated at a desk. A simple backdrop can be made from purchased screens. Many teleprompter software packages are available for computer screen use, or you can use Microsoft PowerPoint.

Computers and Servers

Ask for many electrical outlets and wired computer drops in this area. A desirable plan for electrical outlets is a duplex outlet every three feet, above and below the desk level. Having the computer drops in place eases future expansion. As much as you can, plan for future technology. Some, such as wireless networks, may alleviate the need for pre-wired drops. However, wireless technologies require a consideration of the building's electromagnetic attributes, or the placement of antennas.

Some server computers will undoubtedly be part of the new school technology, and space for these "hidden" assets should be considered along with the power and network wiring that go with them. Consider the ease with which the building design lends itself to being rewired with different types of cables or optical fibers to accommodate future technology, such as video streaming.

Arrange the computers so that all of the screens can be seen from any location in the library media center. The circulation computer needs to be lower so that the wires are not visible. Plan for a pullout computer keyboard and plenty of leg space.

Groundbreaking and Construction Phase

By the time construction begins, much has been decided, but much work remains. The library media specialist must plan, budget, and acquire all the furnishings and materials that the library will have available on the opening day. Ideally, the library media specialist provides input to the budget approval process. Budget plans should include a healthy provision for initial procurements, an extra first-year funding for correcting opening day shortcomings, and a planned development funding level for three to five years thereafter. At that point, an annual budget that supports replacement costs and school population changes should serve.

Continue to review the building plans and take advantage of, or ask for, periodic walk-throughs with the architect and building supervisor. These can help to avoid the kind of construction mistakes that plague buildings long after they are inhabited.

Furnishings

Shop for the best quality and the best price, but always place comfort and durability over price. This is consistent with the goals and long-term efficiency of the library media center. Laminate tabletops with a wood or textured look reduce and hide damage over the years. Fingerprints can be seen easily on a solid-colored laminate, by comparison.

Wood shelving creates a quiet environment, whereas metal shelving is noisy. Buy shelving that has a back, so items are not as easily lost and difficult to retrieve. Purchase extra shelving on wheels so that areas that grow are adjusted easily. The library media center's collection will grow, and shelves on wheels create more room design possibilities. These also can be easily moved aside to accommodate large group activities, such as author visits and book fairs. Buy bookcases with attachments on the ends to provide extra space for displays. Wood dividers can be used in the picture book section to readjust shelves. Bookends should be tall, heavy, and lined with a urethane base, so they do not easily slide out of position. An atlas table allows easy access to oversized materials. Purchase a slant-top reading table for the primary area. Students enjoy looking at the books, plus, it makes a great area to display books. Buy four book trucks—one each for picture books, fiction books, and nonfiction books, as well as an extra one to load items from the book drop or hold materials pulled for classrooms.

The circulation desk should be no more than 32 inches high so that the youngest patron can be seen. Specify a wood laminate or textured laminate on the circulation desk. The book return cart should have a depressible or descending platform. Locks should be placed on the cabinets, drawers, and file cabinets. Purchase the automated catalog system early so that new materials can be quickly loaded onto the server as they arrive.

The technology equipment may include Smart Boards and LCD projectors. Therefore, purchase computers with audiovisual capabilities and an S-video connector so that an audience can view computer projects, as well as video streaming.

Collection Development

Collection development is one of the most important parts of the library media specialist's job. It also is one of the most enjoyable. Catalogs deluge the library media specialist; the variety and quantity is staggering. The question on the lips of many new library media specialists is "Where to begin first?" The following considerations will help establish an enduring and quality collection that serves the mission of the library media center towards its patrons.

Soliciting Input

The first step in building a collection is to become familiar with the school's curriculum. The main goal of a library media center is to enhance student achievement. What better way to accomplish this than by acquiring curriculum-based materials for students and teachers? Ask the principal, the assistant principal, the grade level chairperson, the curriculum committee leadership, and the teachers for input. All parties will appreciate the interest in creating a library media center as a partner in the curriculum focus of the school.

In addition, examine the state curriculum frameworks. Many states have adopted curriculum standards that are accessible via the Internet. Also, copy the table of contents from each of the textbooks as a general guide to the curriculum. Keep a clipboard at the circulation desk for teacher and student recommendations.

Many vendors have packages for the opening day collection. They usually use a percentage breakdown of the number of materials to purchase for each category and Dewey classification number. Figure 1.1 shows the author's recommended distribution.

Figure 1.1: Distribution of Materials for Elementary School Libraries

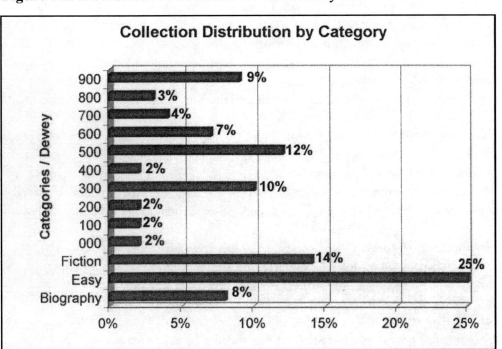

Purpose of Materials

Does the material focus on curriculum objectives? Does it add value to the library media center collection? Materials speak to areas of study, but also to the enrichment of students' lives. Materials in the library media center collection should address childhood problems and issues. Character development and multicultural materials add to the worth of the collection. Materials in the dominant language and any smaller primary language groups of the student population are important.

Timelessness

Does the material stand the test of time? Is its appeal going to last through generations of students? The timelessness of material is judged by its message. The message needs to be universal and eternal. Does it provide a rich context of meaning for the student? In some cases, the material provides historical reference and insight into characters' feelings and problems.

Quality of Content

Build a collection based on quality. Purchase materials from award lists, such as Caldecott, Newbery, Jane Addams, and Coretta Scott King Award. Search magazines for starred reviews. *The School Library Journal, Booklist, The Horn Book Magazine,* and *LMC: Library Media Connection Magazine* are some magazines that review new materials.

Readability

Is the material easy to read? Check to see if the language flows from one section or chapter to another. Does the nonfiction work present clear, stated objectives? Do the illustrations provide emphasis and clarity to the words?

Authority of Information

Authority is important in nonfiction materials. The author must have the education and background to write on the subject. Check to see if the author has written other books on the subject.

Cultural and Social Biases

Are diverse culture groups depicted in a positive manner? Are gender roles stereotypical or free of bias? Do the photographs and illustrations depict diverse people groups?

Reputation of Author/Publisher

Is the publisher noted for its expertise in a subject area? Is the publishing house known for its quality in literature?

Quality of Binding

Select binding quality over price when ordering books. Avoid discounted, cheaply bound materials. Look for strength and durability. Paper quality also is important. Thin sheets of "paperback" quality paper will not last.

Selection Tools

Use library resources to build a great collection. Several reference books have been written to enable the library media specialist to quickly survey materials (for a bibliographic list, see Appendix B: Resources to Build Elementary Library Media Center Collections):

- *Children's Catalog*
- *Best Books for Children: Preschool Through Grade 6*
- *The Elementary School Library Collection: A Guide to Books and Other Media Adventuring with Books*
- *Children's Books from Other Countries*
- *Selecting Books for the Elementary School Library Media Center*
- *Picture Books by Latino Writers: A Guide for Librarians, Teachers, Parents, and Students*

Special Language Collections

Any non-English language, bilingual, or ESL (English as a second language) collection should follow all of the basic rules of collection development previously listed, plus the following criteria:

- **Information** Is the information about the culture accurate and positive?
- **Characters** Are the culture's characters in passive or active roles? An active role is preferred.

- **Plot** Is the plot recognizable by different populations? Is there a single, universal concept that is familiar to all readers of any language or culture?
- **Illustrations** Are they stereotyped, or do they reflect the cultural heritage of the people group?
- **Translation** If the material is a translation, is it superior in quality and suitable for children?

Spanish is a major language group throughout the United States. The same issues, of course, apply to other language groups, although book selection may be more limited. Many major vendors list Spanish, bilingual, and ESL selections. The following is a list of several specialized publishers who offer a more diverse selection of materials (see Appendix C: Spanish Language, Bilingual, and English as a Second Language (ESL) Publishers for addresses and Web sites):

- **Cinco Punto Press** offers titles for early readers, middle readers, and bilingual needs, as well as some audiovisual materials. Its excellent Web site offers creative exercises to encourage new speakers to try a different language.
- **Me+Mi Publishing, Inc.** specializes in bilingual early concept books for infants and toddlers.
- **Santillana USA** is dedicated to "disseminating the very best Spanish language literature throughout the United States."
- **Multi-Cultural Books and Videos** offers a wide selection of materials for many languages. MARC records are available.
- **Los Andes Publishing Company** has been in existence for 12 years and has garnered awards for its catalog.

School Library Journal and *Publishers Weekly* jointly publish *Criticas, an English Speaker's Guide to the Latest Spanish Language Titles*. The magazine features critical reviews of adult and children's materials. The magazine's Web site features an issue archive as well as links to other Spanish language publishers.

The Professional Collection

The professional collection is both a resource for the school's professional staff and an opportunity for teachers and the library media specialist to explore new ideas and create collaborations. Staff suggestions and examples gleaned from background research will provide leads about materials to include in the professional collection.

Many library media specialists contract a subscription service for their magazines. Providers offer discounts for volume sales. See Appendix D: Directory of Subscription Service Providers for more details.

Suggested magazines for teachers include the following (see Appendix E: Suggested Periodical Titles for Teachers for addresses):

- *Copycat Magazine*
- *Mailbox Magazine*; *Teacher's Helper*; *Mailbox Bookbag* — from The Education Center
- *Teaching Pre-K–8*

- *The Reading Teacher*
- *R T W Magazine (Reading Writing Thinking)* — available in print and online versions
- *Book Links: Connecting Books, Libraries, and Classrooms*
- *Instructor Magazine*

Audiovisual Materials

The selection policy for audiovisual materials is similar to the policy for books, with a few differences:

- **Technical Quality** Does the media producer present the subject in a visually pleasing format? Does the producer have a reputation for the production of superior media? Use media reviews found in *School Library Journal* for guidance.
- **Format** Make budget allowances for media format obsolescence.
- **Medium** Which medium is most suitable for the subject and the viewers?
- **Appropriateness** Does the material meet age level requirements of the school? Usually, library video supply companies will specify a grade level in their catalogs. If not, view the material before distribution to the school.

Audiovisual Equipment

When ordering audiovisual equipment for a new school, evaluate items that other recently built schools in the district have ordered. Following is a list of the author's list of desirable equipment:

- Audio players for cassettes and DVDs
- Computer for checking out materials
- Computer for library office use
- Computers for student use (8–10)
- Digital camcorder
- Digital cameras (3)
- Laptop computers with built-in ether card
- LCD projector
- Overhead projectors for teachers, plus a supply of 2 bulbs for each
- Printers (2)
- Scanner
- Smart Board
- TV carts (Do not order tall carts that can easily tip over.)
- TVs (1 per teacher)
- VCR or DVD player (1 for each teacher)
- Video cameras (2)
- Wireless equipment

Library Supplies

The right supplies make the library media center run smoothly. Library supply companies, such as Demco, Highsmith, and The Library Store, offer catalogs in print form as well as online. To make life easier, use the following essential supply list:

- 3M Scotch 845™ Book Tape in various sizes
- Antiseptic wipes for quick cleanup of surfaces and hands
- Barcode and spine labels
- Binders with clear front covers
- Blank video and audiotape cassettes—30-, 60-, 90-, and 120-minute length tapes
- Bone folders
- Book reinforcement corners
- Bookmarks
- CD-RW (compact disc on which programs can be written)
- Clean cover gel (a gentle material to clean sticky book covers)
- Corrective liquid
- Filmoplast™ tape (does not discolor over time)
- Goo-Gone™
- Headphones for audiocassettes
- "In and Out" plastic shelves
- Laminate for paperback books
- Magazine boxes
- Mailing supplies—envelopes of various sizes
- Manila folders—plain and colored
- Markers, pens, and pencils
- Norbond™ Adhesive (a tough, flexible liquid glue for repairing spines of books)
- Notepads
- Paper—plain, colored, and card stock
- Paper hinge tape
- Paperclips—large and small
- Pencil holders
- Plastic covers for magazines
- Plastic media storage bags with hooks, such as Monaco™
- Plastic storage boxes in various sizes
- Power strips
- Printer ribbons
- Projection lamps and bulbs for audiovisual equipment
- Rack to hold big books and media audiocassettes
- Rubber bands, 4-way (to hold books tight while the glue dries)
- Scissors
- Sheets of label stickers
- Stamps—property stamp and address stamp
- Staplers
- Tape—masking tape, clear everyday tape, and packaging tape
- Tape dispensers

Before and After School Opening

As the initial school opening approaches, the librarian can take steps to enhance and define the role of the library media center in the life of the school. The administration and staffing of the classrooms will be taking shape, and the student population, hopefully, will be settled before the ending of school the previous year. Find out which schools will send students to the new school, and visit them. Meet the incoming students. Ask them what they like to read. Try to identify issues specific to your soon-to-be school population. Study the student demographics with regard to language and culture groups and any other facts that might help direct acquisition decisions.

Meet with the teachers, and ask about their curriculum focus. Let them know that the library media center is there to help in the instruction process. Give them a card with an e-mail address and phone number so that they can relay information about resources needed for the library media center.

The local community and parents will likely share an excitement about the opening of a new school, so this will be an opportunity to build bridges for their involvement. Plan and state clearly how gifts and donations will be accepted according to the library selection policy. At outreach or visitation events, let potential donors know about the policy. Meanwhile, explain that some materials might be donated to classroom libraries. Re-routing donations occurs when materials are duplicated or the quality of binding doesn't meet the standards of the selection policy. Send a letter to parents before the school opens, and let them know help is needed to stock the shelves with new books for their children. Describe the library media center's needs during the school year, too. (See Chapter 11 for more details about fostering good relationships with volunteers.)

School Opening

Student and Faculty Orientations

The opening weeks of school are always exciting, especially for a new school. Meet with teachers before the students arrive on campus, but be aware that they also will be rushing to prepare first days in the classroom. The orientation period is an opportunity to get the bugs ironed out in the system while enlisting cooperation on procedures.

Scheduling

Lobby early for a flexible schedule. Flexible scheduling defines the role of the library media specialist as that of a consultant and a collaborator. Information skills and research lessons are taught at the point of need, and the library media specialist is a partner with the classroom teacher. Relevant materials are gathered for classroom research projects. The library media specialist plans objectives, activities, and evaluation tools with the teacher. Fixed scheduling results in missed opportunities to impact student learning. A rigid schedule does not allow for the planning and designing of valuable instruction with the teacher. Do not be fooled by the "modified flexible plan," which locks in classes to a fixed schedule and allows time when classes are not in the library media center to be scheduled as "flexible scheduled time." The plan might look something like Figure 1.2.

Figure 1.2: Modified Flexible Schedule

	MONDAY	TUESDAY	WEDNESDAY	THURSDAY	FRIDAY
8:00 - 8:30		KINDERGARTEN	KINDERGARTEN	KINDERGARTEN	
8:30 - 9:00		KINDERGARTEN			
9:00 - 10:00		FIRST GRADE	FIRST GRADE	FIRST GRADE	
10:00 - 10:30		SECOND GRADE	SECOND GRADE		
10:30 - 11:00					
11:00 - 11:30		THIRD GRADE		THIRD GRADE	THIRD GRADE
11:30 - 12:00	LUNCH	LUNCH	LUNCH	LUNCH	LUNCH
12:00 - 12:30	FOURTH GRADE	FOURTH GRADE	FOURTH GRADE	FOURTH GRADE	
12:30 - 1:00		FIFTH GRADE			
1:00 - 1:30	FIFTH GRADE		THIRD GRADE	FIFTH GRADE	
1:30 - 2:00					
2:00 - 2:30				SECOND GRADE	
2:30 - 3:00					
	FLEXIBLE TIME				

Indeed, this type of schedule may exist as a compromise when the principal and staff have not accepted a flexible schedule for the library media center. The modified flexible plan prevents planning with teachers and curriculum teams. In reality, teachers do not plan according to the library media specialist's schedule; they plan with their team according to their own schedule. A truly flexible schedule is "curriculum-driven." A flexible library schedule might look like the example in Figure 1.3 on page 14. Keep in mind that a flexible schedule will change from week to week, and the example displays only one week.

Responding to Feedback

Adopt a "can do" attitude. Be ready to try any project the administrator and staff requests. The tone set by the library media specialist in the first year creates a lasting impression among students, parents, faculty, and administrators.

Figure 1.3: True Flexible Schedule

AM	MONDAY	TUESDAY	WEDNESDAY	THURSDAY	FRIDAY
	8:00 – 9:40 Grade 5 - State project	**8:00 – 9:30** Grade 5 – State project	**8:00 – 9:00** Grade 5 – State project	**8:00 – 8:30** Genre booktalks Grade 4 - Liu	**8:50 – 9:40** Team Meeting – Grade 1 – Penguin project – room 123
	10:00 – 10:30 Storytime K- Smith	**10:00 – 10:50** Team meeting with grade 4 – Room 110	**10:20 – 10:50 –** Genre booktalks Grade 4 – Doe	**10:00 – 11:00** Grade 2 – reading groups	
		11:15 – 11:45 Storytime – Grade 1 - Brown	**11:35 – 12:05** Storytime - K– Noble	**11:10 – 11:50** Team meeting with grade 2 - LMC	**11:50 – 12:30** grade 5 – evaluation of state project LMC
PM	**1:00 – 1:30** Storytime – K Williams **2:00 – 2:30** Storytime Grade 1 - Lee	**1:30 – 2:30** Storytime – Grade 1 - Gonzales	**1:40 – 2:10** Genre booktalks Grade 4 - Page	**1:00 – 1:30** Storytime – K Doyle	**1:00 – 2:00** Grade 2 -reading groups

Things That Go Wrong and How to Cope

The first year in a new school is fraught with mistakes and glitches. At times you may feel overwhelmed as you attempt to get used to new students, a new administrator, and problems with equipment. Do not be surprised if the building construction or furnishing deliveries or any other aspect of this large project does not go exactly as planned. Flexibility and a positive attitude will save the day.

Chapter 2

Starting Over: The Library Media Specialist in a New School District

This chapter is devoted to the library media specialist who moves from one school district to another, whether it is in the same state or a different state. He or she is leaping from a deep pool of familiarity to an ocean of the unknown. Sometimes a foundation of expertise makes the trip smoother. More often, it is time to buckle up for a bumpy ride.

In a one-person library media center, the library media specialist is often expected to perform immediately at a high level of service, with little or no orientation to the new district and school. In this chapter, tips and inside wisdom make the new assignment as painless as possible.

Finding a Mentor

Many school districts provide an experienced teacher as a mentor for new teachers, but a mentor for the librarian often does not exist. If this is the case, quickly take a look around for a friendly face among the librarians at other schools in the new district. Ask if he or she would be willing to form a mentor relationship. Consider joining the LM_NET listserv <http://ericir.syr.edu/lm_net/>. It is a great way to be connected with librarians around the world. Search the archives at LM_NET by topic to find helpful suggestions and answers to many library media center problems. Another source for help is the American Library Association (ALA). The ALA Web site <http://www.ala.org/> provides news of upcoming events, legislative initiatives, and copyright information. The ALA Library Web page lists an online and conventional periodicals list with purchase information, links to other library resources, library fact sheets, and an archive. The ALA also hosts a New Member Round Table at <http://www.ala.org/Content/NavigationMenu/Our_Association/Round_Tables/ NMRT/NMRT.htm>. This group is open to ALA members who have been library media specialists less than 10 years. Stay in touch with other new members on the discussion list (NMRT-L). Members discuss areas of importance to librarians who need answers. However, it is not archived.

The Function and Design of the Library Media Center

A Multipurpose Space

Accommodating multiple functions is an important consideration of space design for the library media center. The library media center has many different functions: reading, storytelling, small and large group research, faculty meetings, book fairs, and circulation. Faculty meetings are held in the library media center because it is one of the largest spaces on campus. Be flexible in creating space and obliging group requests. When more groups use the library media center, more people view the library program's success. Bulletin boards that attest to student learning and successful reading program results can promote the library.

Flow of People

Check the traffic pattern in the library. Mentally mark the obstacles that people encounter when entering the library media center and accessing the materials on the shelves. Shelves that can be rearranged easily are a plus. If the shelves are fixed and cannot be rearranged, take a look at the library's tables and chairs. Could another arrangement improve access to the shelves?

The Interior Design

Look at the library media center's interior design. Bring in plants and new posters, or order soft sculptures for the walls. Vendors such as Demco and Highsmith offer many options for library reading centers.

Make signs to designate different areas in the library media center. To construct a simple stand for holding a sign, use hot glue to attach a 12-inch by $3/8$-inch wood dowel stick to a circular wood base with a drilled hole. Then use the hot glue to attach a clothespin with the jaws up at the top end of the dowel stick. Spray paint the stand in school colors.

Have fun decorating to promote reading. Experiment with themes, especially in the storytime area. Here are some themes to try:

- **School Mascot** Locate posters, soft sculptures, or plastic models of your school mascot. Shop garage sales and novelty stores to find inexpensive materials.
- **Garden** Paint simple flowers and sky on the wall, and place white picket garden boards against the wall. Buy a patio chair and a chaise

lounge. Students can pretend they are listening to stories under a shady tree in the backyard.

- **Rain Forest** Bundle craft paper together to make trees, and cut green craft paper as the leaves. Purchase puppets and dangle them from the trees. Whenever one is needed, simply pull it from the tree. Students delight in guessing which one is used for storytime.
- **Castle** Use wallpaper border, and paint ornate cornices and columns. "The Storytime Queen/King" becomes the library media specialist's new title. Paint an old chair with gold paint. Beside the golden chair, place a treasure box that holds each day's storybook and a puppet to share with the students.

The Office

The office space may be a shelf in one corner of the library, a desk in one end of the audiovisual area, or a color-coordinated, large workspace. Whatever the shape and size of the office, claim it. Hang a favorite painting or poster. Place favorite family photos on the desk. Now to begin the next big job: the file cabinets.

Within well-organized manila folders are answers to many of the library media specialist's most difficult questions. Proceed slowly and with full attention to detail as you survey the previous librarian's filing system. Hopefully, he or she left behind previous years' book fair results, inventory reports, and purchase orders. Examine carefully how each report is completed. Make note of which forms are used, and request them from the school secretary. Locate receipt books. These are necessary when students return lost books from summer vacation. Having receipt books for each area of bookkeeping, such as Lost Books, Library Fines, and Birthday Book Club donations, can be helpful.

Take a break and examine how each file drawer is organized. The reason for doing this is simple: when focusing on the content in each file folder, keeping an eye on the overall organization in each drawer can be difficult. Files can be arranged with many variations. Keep all files for the first year, and save the discarding for next year. Create a filing system that is quick and easy to remember. Some filing systems are alphabetical, such as Author Visits, Bookkeeping Receipts, and Computer Service Agreements. Other filing systems are subject-based and color-coded. For example, green folders are used for any type of purchasing or bookkeeping items, yellow folders for author visits and lesson plans; red for reading programs; blue for items sent for repairs, equipment manuals, or service agreements. Each color-coded file is placed in subject-coded hanging folders.

Weeding

Look carefully at the shelves and audiovisual materials area. Are some of the AV items or equipment outdated or obsolete? Is the area crowded with materials that are no longer used? Are book covers damaged and pages torn?

Shelved Materials

When space on the shelves grows tighter and tighter, it is time to practice the delicate art of weeding. Weeding, or deselection as it is sometimes called, is the library term used for a systematic removal of items to ensure that the library media center materials are current and useful. Incomplete, outdated information misleads students. Removing dated, damaged items creates a collection that is more attractive to patrons. Space is often at a premium, so the weeding process is very important. Check to see if the school district has a weeding policy. In the weeding process, materials are examined with emphasis placed upon any strong or weak points, gaps, saturated areas, and the needs of the learning community. For assistance, try using the acronym that I devised: AEIOU. Each letter provides a clue about a question to ask:

- **Attractive** Is the material attractive, or is it worn and beyond repair?
- **Expendable** Does the item have value, either literary or scientific? Do other items on the shelf contain better formats with the same information?
- **Improved** Has a later edition improved the information in the item?
- **Outdated** Is the information outdated or misleading?
- **User** Do the users prefer particular materials? Does the community favor certain genres, titles, local authors, or subjects?

During the first year on a new assignment, weeding is probably the last item on the "To Do" list. In every library collection, small or large, quality needs to be the focus. Weeding is a satisfying experience as a library media specialist reshapes the collection to fit the community's needs. No time to fit weeding in an already busy schedule? You can weed in two separate periods: 1) Set aside time when the library is free of classes to examine just one shelf, and mark items for repair, rebinding, reordering, and weeding. 2) Use the AEIOU method daily as the patrons check in their items. Purchase a pack of three by five inch index cards. Mark the items and slip the card into the book or attach it to the media package. Deposit the items into labeled, plastic bins. At the end of the day, check out the items to their own specific category, such as Bindery, Repair, or Discard. Print a list of these user categories at the end of the year so that they are accounted for during inventory.

Audiovisuals

During the first year, observe which materials are circulating. Some filmstrips might be favorites that teachers use year after year. Discard the ones that are not used, and purchase videotapes or DVDs that have the same or comparable information. Locate all the equipment manuals and warranty agreements. Check for equipment that needs to be repaired. Ask the school secretary about the procedure for tagging an item for discard or repairs.

Evaluating Previous Library Service

The job as the new library media specialist on the campus is to discover ways that student learning can be positively impacted while cultivating satisfaction among the faculty, staff, parents, and students. This is a huge assignment. There is no guarantee that you will make everyone happy. Nevertheless, do not try to imitate the previous library media specialist. Everyone has his or her own personal style of service. The best first step is to find out, as accurately as possible, the expectations of the administration and the patrons.

An excellent resource for ascertaining needs in the library media center is *Information Power: Building Partnerships for Learning* (American Library Association, 1998) and its accompanying workbook, *A Planning Guide for Information Power* (American Library Association, 1999). First, measure the library media center against the national standards for libraries. The standards are included in *Information Power*. Next, survey the students to determine usage and attitudes in the library media center. The American Association of School Librarians (AASL) has created three student surveys to complete online once you have e-mailed the AASL Office to obtain the state and school code; you do not need to spend hours of valuable time creating a new survey from scratch. The Power Reader Survey is broken down into two categories: kindergarten through fourth grade, and fifth grade through eighth grade. The Power Learner Survey is specifically designed for students to respond to after completing a research lesson in the library. The e-mail address is *aasl@ala.org*. The Power Reader and Power Learner Student Surveys are available at <http://www.ala.org/aasl/action/index.html>. Once the data is in hand, it is time for the real challenge: to explore the survey results and make decisions.

Library Advisory Committee

Forming the Committee

It is difficult for the library media specialist alone to make informed decisions for the library media center. This is where the school's learning community plays an important role. This community consists of teachers, students, administration, parents, and other adults, such as business people and community leaders. The library media specialist forms a Library Advisory Committee with these partners to achieve a mutual goal: creating information-literate students. The Library Advisory Committee not only learns a great deal about the library media center, but also becomes its biggest champion. Choose at least four or five persons from the learning community representing each area: teachers, administrators, parents, other adults, and students who are familiar with the library's current service. Include the campus technology facilitator on the committee if the position exists. Expertise in library science is not a requirement for members, simply an interest in the impact of the library media center. Ask for a commitment of once a quarter, and schedule the meetings after school. During the first, hectic year, form the committee after the winter break. It takes time to learn who the library supporters are when working in a new school.

The Committee Meeting Process

1. Provide an agenda sheet with room for note taking. If the notes of the Library Advisory Committee will be sent to administrators, delegate one person at each meeting to take notes.

2. Create a mission statement. The first job the committee should tackle is the mission statement for the school library. A good starting place is to examine the school's mission statement and determine how the library media center supports it. Demonstrate any survey results gathered from local and national sources that show accomplishment and areas that need improvement. Begin the mission statement process by brainstorming ideas and examining other school's mission statements. Set pen to paper and post the library's mission statement in the library and on the school's Web page. Inform the staff and administrators through e-mail or notes.

3. Set library goals. The next item for the committee to determine is the library media center's goals. Goals are broad, far-reaching statements. A goal looks to the present and future of the library. The committee members bring a variety of interests to the Library Advisory Committee. The newly created mission statement reflects their various perspectives, which is exactly what is needed.

4. Determine objectives. Objectives are the concrete and measurable steps to be taken to carry out goals. Consider objectives as the "walking feet" of the goals for the library media center. They also are time-sensitive. Formulating objectives requires the Library Advisory Committee to reflect and analyze the data gathered from the surveys. A good objective should have two parts: a verb phrase followed by an operation phrase. For example:

    Goal: Provide current science materials for access by students and faculty.

    Objective: The library media specialist consults (verb phrase) with the science lead teacher and grade level teachers over the next three months (operation phrase) to determine science materials that are needed in the library media center.

    The library media specialist selects and purchases (verb phrase) new science books and media over the next three years (operation phrase).

5. Develop the action plan. After the goals and objectives are set, the Library Advisory Committee breathes life into the library program via the action plan. The action plan specifies how the learning community accomplishes the objectives with the resources on hand. Some of the action plans are within the scope of the library media specialist and staff or volunteers. Other action plans involve the administration, faculty, and parents. Here is an example of an action plan based on the goal and objective listed previously:

    Action Plan: The library media specialist will spend X dollars each year for the next three years to purchase new science materials. The money for the new materials will be generated by activities promoted by the PTA.

6. Refine the action plan. Future meetings can be devoted to making the action plan a practical, effective document. The library media specialist considers the action plan developed by the Library Advisory Committee and determines which items will be implemented. Are some of the actions short-term? Are others long-range, but need to be implemented soon? The quarterly meetings can be a progress report from this point.

A school library media center is always growing and changing. Student populations change as the district realigns the boundaries that each school supports. A change in administration and staff can affect the focus of the library. The library media specialist can weather changes more easily when he or she has the support of the Library Advisory Committee rather than going it alone.

Inherited Programs from Your Predecessor

The new library media specialist often inherits programs in the established school. These programs may be school-wide events and fund raisers. The inheritance might be a reading program. Feedback from the faculty, parents, and students reveals the success or problems of the event or program.

One library media specialist was faced with an after-hours program that entailed a great deal of work. The program involved bringing 20 prominent people into the school to read to students one evening.

"I had always dabbled in storytelling, so why not turn it into a storytelling event," commented Beth. "I went to the Internet and keyed in 'storytellers' and found a site that was a directory to storytelling guilds around the country. I found my geographic area and called the contact person. She presented it to the guild, and I received quite a few storytellers. It still was not enough people. I decided to form a storytelling group within the school made up of students. I chose fourth graders because at our school fifth graders are in charge of the daily school broadcast. I talked to the fourth grade teachers, and they all agreed it would be a great idea. I scheduled a class with each teacher. I read a folktale to the students. Then I asked simple questions, such as 'Would this be a good story to tell?' and 'Why do you think so?' Most of them responded with the fact that it had several repetitive phrases and they saw the pictures in their imaginations. The teachers gave me names of those students who were interested and also comfortable in front of large groups."

"The storytelling group and I met once a week," Beth continued. "At the first meeting, each student chose one story to tell. They were instructed to read the story several times, practice, and then audition at the end of the month. Later in the year, we met two or three times a week during their afternoon recess. It was an amazing success," Beth concluded. The storytelling event now replaces the original concept. (See Chapter 6 for more details about organizing a storytelling festival.)

Managing reading programs, collaborating with teachers, and completing the many clerical duties is overwhelming. Finding time to squeeze it all in is very difficult. Librarians must schedule a regular "administrative" time slot each day in which fewer classes are scheduled in the library media center. Mark the time slots for the administrative duties on the weekly library media center calendar. Administrative time can be used by the lone librarian to catch up on some of the enormity of paperwork and the many tasks that make up the library media specialist's day.

Here are some examples of how to use the administrative time:

- Catalog materials
- Check in and shelve materials
- Locate materials for teachers
- Order materials
- Perform inventory
- Plan collaboration lessons with teachers
- Publish a newsletter or work on the library media center Web page
- Search Web sites to find information for teachers
- Update budget items
- Weed materials

Introducing Yourself

To Staff

Before the new school year begins, place a bookmark in each staff member's mailbox with a brief note of introduction. Include a brief biography, and list any hobbies. Let the faculty and staff know that assistance with their curricular needs and collaboration ideas is a top priority. Try hard not to refuse a request, especially an urgent material request. Inform the faculty that a few days' notice is needed by the library media specialist to fill requests. However, some of the staff have difficulty remembering this, whether they are experienced, veteran teachers or ones who graduated yesterday. Instead of being negative and refusing every last-minute request, state that every effort will be made to complete it—and mean it. Do let them know that more time would be preferable. Fill the request quickly, and vow next year to ease changes into place. Design a materials request form like the one in Figure 2.1. Discuss the form via e-mail or a faculty meeting. Place a few forms in each teacher's box.

Making a change can be especially difficult if the preceding library media specialist held the position for many years. The staff may expect the same level and style of service as the predecessor. Becoming an integral part of the faculty takes time. Eat lunch in the teacher's lounge, and become acquainted with the faculty. Ask to be a part of a team, if not assigned one. New friendships add richer meaning to personal and work life. Building relationships develops into the basis for collaboration partnerships.

To Students

Be prepared for astonished looks as students ask, "Where's Mr./Ms. _____ ?" An explanation may be needed, as well as the answer to the question "Why?" It takes time to create an impression and build trust with students. In the attempt to establish a new program, the new librarian will probably hear this comment: "Mr./Ms. _____ let us (fill in the blank)." Respond with the comment "Well, things have changed." By mid-year, the student comments about the

Figure 2.1: Materials Request Form

Materials Request Form

Teacher name: _____

Grade level: _____

Subject:

    Fiction ☐   Nonfiction ☐   Both ☐

Media type: (circle one)   Audiocassette   Videocassette   DVD   CD-ROM   Other

Titles _____

       _____

       _____

       _____

When do you need the materials?

The librarian can help with

    Planning together   Teaching material   Evaluating the project predecessor subside. Try creating a bulletin board to speed up the introduction process. Include photographs of family, pets, and hobbies. Add a written list of favorite books. Include a picture from elementary school days on the bulletin board.

To Parents

An "Open House" or "Meet the Teacher" night is a good avenue to advertise the library program. Parents do not usually visit the library. Give them a reason to stop by. Open the doors wide for people to drift into the library media center. Stand by the door and offer free bookmarks to entice visitors. Hold a puppet and give out bookmarks to younger children. The event can be "show and tell" time on a grand scale. Create a small, colorful brochure about the library media center. Produce a PowerPoint presentation to be continuously looped on a computer monitor screen or projected via a television. Create a sign-up list for potential volunteers. A positive attitude and an attractive library draw people in the door and hopefully onto the volunteer sheet. Parents make good public relations personnel when they volunteer in the library media center. (See Chapter 11 for more information about volunteers.)

To the Parent Teacher Association

Attend the PTA meetings to become acquainted with the students' parents. Try to participate in every special event the organization sponsors. Be present for every Chili Supper and Spaghetti Supper. Your role as a library media specialist should be one of a constant enthusiast for the library program. The more visible the library media specialist, the more the parents recognize that this person cares for their children and the school. Parent-teacher organizations raise money for special projects, and seeing a smiling face consistently at a few meetings will benefit the library program.

Becoming Indispensable

Volunteer for the key committees on the campus. Ask to be on the Leadership Committee, Technology Committee, or Grant Writing Committee. Some districts have Site-Based Committees, which work on local issues for each campus. These committees are where the big decisions are made about the school. The reason for joining is obvious—promotion of the library program. It bears repeating: the library media specialist is the champion and promoter of the library, day in and day out. Information about recent grant efforts, the latest budget and district news, and acquaintance with members of the school's learning community are a few of the benefits of joining the campus leadership team.

"Mistake" Is My Middle Name

Perfectionism is forbidden in the first year of a new assignment or any year, for that matter. Striving for it is an elusive desire. You'll soon realize that you will never be able to achieve it. Mistakes are bound to happen. The good news is that mistakes can be viewed positively. They are part of the boot camp experience of that first year.

"I was to make a presentation before an important librarians' group during a job interview," Diane related. "I had my PowerPoint presentation set to go with wonderful graphics and stellar information. A few days before the meeting, I developed a throat infection. The date could not be moved, so I showed up with disk in hand and a body full of cough medications. I am nervous before adults, and the quality of my voice that day was poor, to say the least. I had a specific time period to convince these people I was the one for the job. During the presentation I had a coughing fit. They kindly offered me water. I made a sweeping gesture, and you guessed it, knocked over the water near the laptop. The water didn't land on the laptop. However, my audience was affected. Several people ran outside to get paper towels and urged me to keep going to keep within the time limit. Miraculously, I finished and managed to slink out of the interview, with body and soul somewhat intact. I did not get the job. Later, I had a good laugh and promised myself some good would come out of the experience. What did I learn? I learned that if necessary, beg for another interview and refuse all offers of liquid refreshment during presentations," a wiser Diane noted.

Give yourself permission to say, "I'm new here," whenever something goes wrong. So many things are different in a new school district. Instructions on procedures might have to be heard more than once. Make that several times. At the end of the year, carve out some reflection time to think about all the ups and downs. Then, wonder in amazement at all that has been accomplished. A pat on the back and a dinner out complete the "reward" ceremony. Survival is at hand, but more than that, a measure of confidence and competence is now present to begin the next year.

Chapter 3

Time Management and the Library Media Center

Symptoms of the Time Management-Challenged

- Is work piling up higher and higher on your desk?
- Are you juggling more and more tasks and dropping a few along the way?
- Do you drag home exhausted from each day?
- Do you find yourself re-teaching the same thing over and over?
- Does your principal ignore all requests for assistance?

If the answer to the above questions is a resounding "yes," this chapter will help alleviate some of the panic and confusion from each day. What can help the library media specialist to rise above the mundane and fully understand the powerful mission of the library media center? Certainly, the issue of how to manage the time is foremost. Without an opportunity to see beyond the moment, long-range goals cannot come to fruition because one has no energy left to focus upon them. Thus, one becomes a juggler of time and tasks.

What Is the Problem?

Multitasking is a time management issue. Finding time to take care of the mountain of clerical duties, to train a high school student to shelve books, and to make library services known to the rest of the school are just a few of the many demands you will face. A feeling of floundering, a backlog in tasks, and the habit of procrastination are all signs that you need help with time management. People become procrastinators for many reasons. Sometimes the overtaxed library media specialist just does not know where to start. The tasks are too many and too complicated. The tasks may be unpleasant. Fear of failure stops many people from taking control of their jobs. Postponing a task until it goes away is not reality. Unfortunately, those little unpleasant tasks do not magically disappear. Acknowledge the feelings, and begin steps to adopt a new attitude. Your success and emotional health are at stake.

The Reluctant Time Manager

Maybe time management just sounds too hard. "Learning new time management techniques sounds like a waste of time," an inner voice whispers. These negative voices are the adversary of change. Examine the following negative statements, which are restated from Andrew Berner's article, "The Importance of Time Management in the Small Library."

"Managing time interferes with my creativity."

The truth is the library media specialist can improve creativity by alleviating tedious tasks. Managing time results in freedom for the truly creative exercise of the art of librarianship. Better time management equals more time for the fundamental and creative aspects of the library media specialist's job: assisting students, sharing stories, conducting research classes, and collaborating with teachers.

"I'm too tired to learn about managing my time better."

When faced with each task, ask, "Is this efficient use of time?" Sometimes too much time and energy is spent on unimportant tasks, with little strength left over for the critical ones. Continuously being distracted from what is important results in little accomplishment. So what demons keep library media specialists from accomplishing the good things they know can happen? Unfortunately, many well-intentioned people, programs, and "conveniences" can thwart goals, simply by eating up time. A good defense against this onslaught is to decide ahead what is important to accomplish this day, this month, and this year. Against this backdrop, let the other tasks take their place. Take time each morning to reflect and list the most important items to complete.

"I'd rather be fishing."

This viewpoint suggests that work is some sort of enormous burden to be endured and should not be made easier. Is this right thinking? Perhaps some small adjustments in beliefs are in order. The focus should always be on the result—satisfying the needs of the school's learning community. If this can be accomplished easily and with fun along the way, everybody wins.

"Neatness is not one of my habits, so count me out."

Does neatness equal good organizational skills? Many of us hope not. Some of the best library media specialists have the messiest offices. It is a sign that work is in progress. Does this mean a messy office is an unspoken requirement? No, but once again the focus is on the result—improved service.

"I am more creative under pressure."

This sentiment is fine, but what about when pressure builds up and takes over? Often, the pressure is generated from within. Some reflection is needed to consider which pressures are realistic and which are out of place. Leaving things to the last minute results in more mistakes. Some of us become our own worst enemies, especially when goals are too broad and unrealistic with respect to time, resources, or people available (Berner, 274–275).

If large goals are overwhelming, focus attention on the smaller, immediate tasks. A slogan for this kind of pressure is "Every journey begins with a single step." Or the mantra of the overwhelmed: "Baby steps, baby steps."

What Is the Solution?

Step One: Plan

Planning is an active, dynamic process. It involves looking to each day with an eye to the future. Planning maps out the road to accomplishing your goals for the library media center.

1. Begin each day by writing down the tasks. If you have software that creates a daily calendar, assign each task to a time slot. The software can produce a message on the computer screen or an alarm bell that serves as a reminder.
2. Next, prepare the daily "To Do" list in a written format.
3. At the end of each day, look over the list, and mark any completed tasks. If jobs remain to be completed, readjust tomorrow's schedule to include them.

Step Two: Define Your Work Style

It is important to understand personal work styles. Some people are most productive working in solitude or in quiet surroundings. Others seem to need a certain level of commotion and activity when working. Discover the environment that is most productive. Use this quality time for demanding tasks: setting goals, developing strategies, cataloging, and ordering materials.

Step Three: Clear Out the Minutiae

Learn how to categorize all of the little tasks of the library media specialist's job. Divide a large white board into four sections. In one box, write down all the tasks that need to be done immediately. Label this section the ASAP (as soon as possible) box. In the second box, place all of the tasks that need to be done by the end of the week. In the next box, write down all the tasks that need to be done by the end of the month. The last box is reserved for things that need to be done by the end of the semester and year. Hang the white board in a prominent place in the workroom where you can review it daily.

One of the biggest time wasters many library media specialists agree upon is shelving. If you have no volunteers or even a part-time assistant, shelving can overwhelm you and occupy too much of your day. Consider instructing students in grades three through six in the basic Dewey Decimal Classification System. Form small groups and ask students to shelve the returned library books. After a certain level of proficiency has been achieved, let each student shelve his or her own returned books each week.

Librarians are often the recipients of a daily deluge of mail (or e-mail). Any tip that helps minimize the time and energy spent on small tasks pays big dividends. Alice H. Yucht, author of "Mailbox Methodology," has a clever idea to handle mail. She recommends dating each item, sorting it by size, and having four file baskets. The four baskets are each labeled in the following manner:

- **Action** memos and announcements
- **Information** bills, invoices, letters, and newsletters
- **Subscription** magazines, standing orders, and packages
- **Sales** brochures, fliers, and catalogs

Keep a trashcan nearby, and fill it with duplicate material or items you cannot afford (Yucht, 14–15). Try keeping a pad and pencil quickly available for new ideas and requests. Often, when the library media specialist walks down the hall to lunch, teachers ask for help or materials. How can one person remember all of this information? Fortunately, some great gadgets are on the market for multitasking, such as a writing pen that records messages or a Palm Pilot. On a simpler note, put a piece of paper in a pocket to write down quick requests.

Respond to letters via a fax machine. Write a response on the page sent by the person or company, and fax it back. This saves time and postage costs.

An automated library system is essential in a one-person, elementary school library media center. The benefit of library automation is improved, quicker access to materials for the library's users. Upper elementary students and teachers can easily learn how to check out their own materials without the library media specialist's presence. This results in freedom for one of the most important jobs—helping others.

Step Four: Know the Library Media Center

What are the goals to be accomplished this year in the library media center? Keep the list short, preferably one page. Then ask, "Are these goals challenging?" When comfortable with the list, prioritize it. Meet with the school principal, and find out his or her vision for the library media center. Make connections between the principal's input and the library's goals. Tweak and refine the final product, and print it out in bold print. Send a copy to the principal for any additions to the list. Post the yearly goals on a wall where you can see them every day. The list does not do any good if it is tucked away in a drawer. After creating your goals, develop a list of measurable performance objectives. Use a calendar to mark off completion dates of the objectives and goals.

Step Five: Find Help

One of the most effective ways to reduce the clerical load is to find help. Help can come in many forms—students, parents, and library school students. Network with other librarians to solve the staffing problem. Perhaps they have new ideas about recruiting and retaining volunteer help. Many elementary school librarians prefer student help to parent help because students are less maintenance. They find that parents require more personal attention than students. Students are sometimes willing to take on many of the mundane chores of the library. Many times, parents become volunteers and find the work too routine and boring. They often prefer working in the classroom with students to shelving books, which is usually the most pressing need in the library. Students do need to be rewarded for their efforts in the library media center. Here are some ideas to try (for more ideas, see Chapter 11):

- Every Friday, give the students candy or healthy snacks, and buy inexpensive gifts for holidays.
- Invite student volunteers to have lunch in the library with a friend. Most students are more than ready to escape the noisy lunchroom.
- Let student helpers spend extra time on computers.
- Let the student helpers be the first to check out popular new books.
- Give the students time to read new magazines.

To recruit parent volunteers, see Figure 10.2 in Chapter 10. Use this form at the beginning of the year to ask for help. Find out the names of parents or grandparents of co-workers. These people could be looking for an outlet in which to serve others.

Attending the first PTA meeting can help you garner more support. Ask for a time slot on the agenda, and present the library's needs, plus some positive experiences. Try placing a sign-up sheet for library help at each PTA meeting. Speak before retirement groups, or advertise in their newsletter to add a few more names to the volunteer list.

Step Six: Publicize the Media Center

Are requests for funds being ignored? Maybe it is time to do something that causes the library program to be noticed. The best way to peak an administrator's interest in the library media center is to go to the community. Ask what the community needs. What problems can the library media center program address? Today's library is really all about caring for the school's learning community. One of the most frequent community needs is time for children. In today's busy world, reading with a child can be neglected. Plan a "Family Reading Night," complete with readers from all walks of life. Present the idea to the administration, and notice the response. Many foundations offer grants to address a community's concerns. The awarding of a grant to help the school's community can fulfill a library media center's mission and gain a bit of publicity for the program.

Frequently marketing the library to the administration and staff is essential. Send the principal a monthly report of all the activity in the library, including monthly statistics and special projects in the planning stages. Share problems, special circumstances, and compliments with the administration. E-mail the staff a list of current Web sites and new materials that are helpful in different curriculum areas.

At the end of the year, prepare an annual report. This document is useful during the library media specialist's evaluation. Report whether the goals have been met, and any results or progress. Some goals take longer than a year to complete.

State the history of the library in the annual report. Include vital statistics, such as the number of student checkouts and reading program results.

Compare the statistics with the previous year's data. Each superintendent of a district has a unique educational focus. State how the library's program addressed the district's focus. Be sure to note any big events, visitors, or contributions to the library during the year. Mention any participation in professional activities that benefited the school. Acknowledge donors and their gifts. Include a financial statement, and use statistics. Include plans for the future. Note any changes to be implemented in the upcoming year. Suggested changes include the inclusion or expansion of reading motivation programs or weeding of outdated material. Package the annual report, and mail it to the library supervisor or director, and the district superintendent.

Step Seven: Avoid Professional and Personal Isolation

Many times, you just do not have time to attend a professional organization's meetings or library conventions. Perhaps the school administration frowns on closing the library for the one-person, elementary library media specialist to attend meetings. Convincing supervisors that training and networking with peers promotes superior library service is a priority that must be approached delicately. Most often, administrators are interested in how such events benefit the school. Mention that library service and programming will be improved, and be specific. Do not be afraid to mention areas of difficulty in the library that could be alleviated by seeking out fellow professionals. Locate a copy of the preliminary program of an upcoming conference. Circle the workshops that you plan to attend, and show this to the school administrator or principal. Explain how these sessions will benefit the library and impact student achievement. Subscribing to journals from associations keeps the library media specialist in touch with current topics and training opportunities. Enroll in a listserv with other library media specialists to learn curriculum ideas and management tips.

Many outsiders have idealized the job of a librarian. It is a terrific job, but people see little of the volume of clerical work that is required. If the library media specialist tries to talk to someone else in the school building about the stress of the job, he or she often is met with a confused look. Many people are shocked by the amount of work. Cataloging, ordering, reports, last-minute requests, equipment to repair, research activities to prepare, collaborative planning time with teachers, computer maintenance, and, in most cases, shelving books are just a few of the overwhelming daily tasks. Each one of these activities takes time. Find a sympathetic soul to talk to, preferably another library media specialist. Do not make it a whining session. If you need advice and help, ask for it.

Carve out time for a healthy lifestyle. It can be as simple as parking the car in the remotest spot in the parking lot. If the day's stress is just too much, take a walk at lunchtime around the school building or the track area. Find hobbies that occupy the whole mind so that mental breaks are possible.

Being healthy in mind and body helps you to meet the daily tasks of the library media specialist's job. Make time to learn successful time management skills. Gain control over some of the daily deluge of paperwork. Juggle well, keep the balance, and know when it is time to stop for the day.

Chapter 4

Budget Secrets

One of the many roles of the library media specialist is the job of managing a budget. Some find it fun; others find it scary. It lurks in the background of most of the activities in the library media center and even beyond the walls. Money is needed to purchase supplies, books, audiovisual resources, equipment, and software so that the library media center program can go forth into the new school year.

All budgets include income (amount of money received) and expenditures (amount spent). The two major types of expenditures are capital and expense. Capital expenditures are usually durable and permanent acquisitions, and have additional costs of upkeep, repair, and replacement. Examples of capital expenditures include audiovisual equipment and furniture. They are nonconsumables and become part of the facility. Expense expenditures are those monies spent in the upkeep, repair, and day-to-day operations. Examples of expense expenditures include books, supplies, audiovisual materials, and periodicals.

A given school or district may categorize items differently from the general definitions of capital and expense provided here. One might think that book acquisitions would be a capital expenditure. However, since this expenditure is recurring annually, acquisitions are usually budgeted as an expense. One could easily argue that computer software and even hardware should be considered an expense because these items have limited practical life. However, computers and their software are generally purchased as capital equipment.

Income can come from many different sources. Perhaps the school PTA raises money to bolster the library acquisitions. These funds can be used for books or for special capital acquisitions, such as video cameras for daily news broadcasts. Other sources include grants or federal programs directed at particular types of expenditures. Activity funds are raised by library media center events or activities, and provide the resources for just about anything not covered by the school or district allocation. Essential core expenses would normally be covered by the school's library allocation. Designating separate accounts for each funding source is important to account for how funds were dispensed and for determining future budget expenses.

Organization of Accounts: Paper and Computer

Paper Copy

Budgets, funding, grants, and purchases all entail many notices, receipts, and packing slips. Having an organized method of handling these bits of paper makes the job of tracking and reporting expenditures manageable, maybe even enjoyable. What follows is a simple organization using a three-ring binder:

- Buy index tabs and label each with the account number and the title of the library account.
- After purchase orders are written, make a copy and place in a colored folder marked PENDING: BUDGET CATEGORY. An example is shown in Figure 4.1. Include any sheets attached with the original purchase order.
- When the order arrives, check off the items, sign the purchase order, and place it in the notebook under the tab marked for the specific budget, such as supplies, books, audiovisual materials, or periodicals, as in Figure 4.1.

Solving the Spreadsheet Mystery

This section is designed for those who have spreadsheet woes. Simple columns and their formulas are designated for ease of use. A common requirement for maintaining a budget is to have columns of expenditures subtracted from funds allocated. This can be done with a pad and pencil. With a few simple formulas, the computer spreadsheet can speed the process faster and eliminate arithmetic errors.

Examine the spreadsheet sample in Figure 4.2. The following boxes decipher each row and column.

Figure 4.1: Binder of PENDING Folders

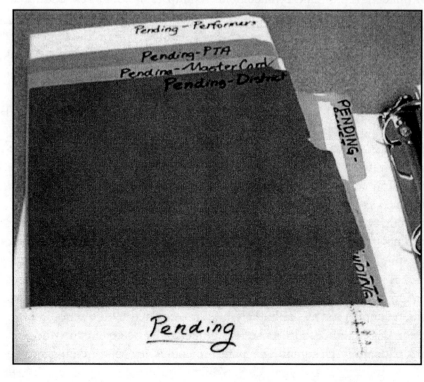

Figure 4.2: Computer Spreadsheet

	A	B	C	D
1	Library Books	Budget Code #	Amount Left:	=D2-SUM(C4:C30)
2			Initial Balance	$4000 (example)
3	Vendor	Date Ordered	Cost	Order Complete?
4	XOX Publishing	8/20/02	$	Yes—9/10/02

Spreadsheet Explanation

ROW ONE:

Column A: State the budget category.

Column B: Specify the budget code, usually a numeric number.

Column C: Type "Amount Left."

Column D: Place the formula that shows how much is left in the account. The example asks that the amount left is equal to the items in column C from row four to thirty subtracted from the initial balance in column D, row two.

ROW TWO:

Row 2 has only two columns in use.

Column C: Type "Initial Balance."

Column D: Type the amount of the original balance in the account. No formulas are required for this row.

ROW THREE:

Column A: List the vendor of the product.

Column B: Type the date when the purchase was requested. Book vendors often take up to three months to fill orders. Note vendors that are slow, and make changes next year.

Column C: Place the total amount of the purchase with any discount subtracted.

Column C: Note whether the order is complete. This serves as a reminder to close out any pending purchase orders.

The rest of the example contains a sample vendor. The same spreadsheet formula can be applied to other budget categories: supply, audiovisual, activity fund, lost books, and so on.

The best safeguard against a possible budget shortfall is the library media specialist's planning efforts the year before it happens. Keep detailed logs, and note the purpose for each purchase. Try to find time each spring before the next year begins to confer with the administrator or principal about projected expenses for the coming year. Before going to the meeting, compile expenses from the current year and notes of any future needs of the faculty, staff, or facilities. Request teachers to record any curriculum areas they have noticed that need to be updated. Perhaps teachers will be covering new material next fall and need materials ordered early to accompany the new curriculum. Observe any audiovisual shortfalls experienced during the previous year. Were there enough videos or DVDs on a particular subject or enough overhead projectors for each classroom? Create a spreadsheet that details expected expenditures, and present it to the administrator during the visit. Make sure the information is clear and prices for projected expenses are accurate.

Marketing the library to the learning community helps to ensure continued financial support from the administration. Tell anyone who will listen the importance the library plays in overall student success and achievement.

Research the results of the 1993 Colorado Study *Impact of School Library Media Centers on Academic Achievement* by Keith Curry Lance, Lynda Welborn, and Christine Hamilton-Pennell. The study was the first to establish that higher test scores are a result of increased spending for school library media programs. These expenditures include additional and more qualified staff members, more time for staff and teacher collaboration, and larger, diverse collections. The study noted that a 10% to 18% gain occurred on the state reading test for students at schools with a large library media center collection, qualified staff, and library programs in place. Key factors in the students' success were the library computers that were linked to classroom computers to enable the students to search quickly for materials. In 2000, a second Colorado study was completed, titled *How School Librarians Help Kids Achieve Standards: The Second Colorado Study* by Keith Curry Lance, Christine Hamilton-Pennell, and Marcia J. Rodney. The second study noticed the impact on reading test scores where networked computers linked school library media centers with classrooms. The higher test scores were related to the number of computers that allowed staff and students to access library media center resources, databases, and the Internet.

Publish both of the Colorado Studies' findings on the school's Web page or in the local paper to show the powerful impact of a well-equipped school library media center. (For information about ordering both Colorado studies, see Appendix G.) Include monthly articles on successful library programs and collaboration efforts within the school. Sponsor a "Research Question of the Month." Photograph the first student to find the correct answer, and interview the student to record how he or she found the answer.

Making Do with Less

Budgets are often slashed regardless of the library media specialist's best efforts to maintain the library in the forefront of the learning community. Following are several ideas in many areas that can help crippled budgets. Note that the library media specialist needs to continue to press for budget support for programs that impact student learning. It is disheartening to return from summer vacation and discover that you have less money to provide more services. Take it as a challenge. At the same time, make notes about deficiencies that occur with less money. For example, in tight budget times, newer materials cannot be purchased. The result is a stagnant collection with inaccurate materials, and students do not have access to current information. Library media clerks are sometimes eliminated in district budget shortfalls. The library media specialist no longer has the time to meet with teachers to plan collaborative efforts and is stretched too thin to cope with the additional clerical duties. In tight economic times, the mood of the school changes. The staff, including the library media specialist, may become fearful of job loss. The result is a distracted, anxious school staff. Technology hardware and software may not be updated in hard times, resulting in a student body that is unprepared to meet the requirements of the workforce.

Materials: Books and Audiovisual

- Peruse the Friday or Saturday edition of the local paper to locate garage sales with toys and books listed. Cruise several neighborhoods to find inexpensive stuffed animals, art objects, and puppets to decorate the library media center. Make it a weekly Saturday expedition to hunt down great bargains.
- Attend the annual book sale of the Friends of the Library group of the local public library. Grab a cart and go early for the best books. You often can purchase well-bound children's books and audiovisual media for a fraction of the original cost. You need to decide if materials purchased without MARC catalog records are worth the time and effort, however.
- Contact the local United States Post Office for nondeliverable items, such as magazines and newspapers. Often, many items are discarded due to the lack of a correct address.
- Let your community know that the library takes gently used book donations. Each time someone brings in a book, issue a ticket for a special treat, such as lunch in the library with a friend.
- Sponsor a "Birthday Book Club." Send home a note with students at the beginning of the school year. Parents who desire to participate send the completed form back to school with funds for a book to be donated to the library in their child's name. Some schools report success with this program, but it has drawbacks. What about the students who are not able to afford birthday books? In addition, the birthday book program often results in more work for the library staff. Use a form, such as the one pictured in Figure 4.3 on page 38 (similar to a design by librarian Meg Beasley). Place the funds in the Library Activity Fund to purchase books for the collection. Have a selection of books on hand for students to choose during the week of their birthday.

A label, such as shown in Figure 4.4 on page 39, can be prepared for placement in the front of each book as a dedication. Ask permission to present the birthday books to the students during school assemblies. Buy a birthday cake headband, and ask one of the students to wear it. The birthday book is checked out to the student before the special presentation. Include a gift of a pencil and food coupon to make it a special occasion.

Figure 4.3: Birthday Book Club Form

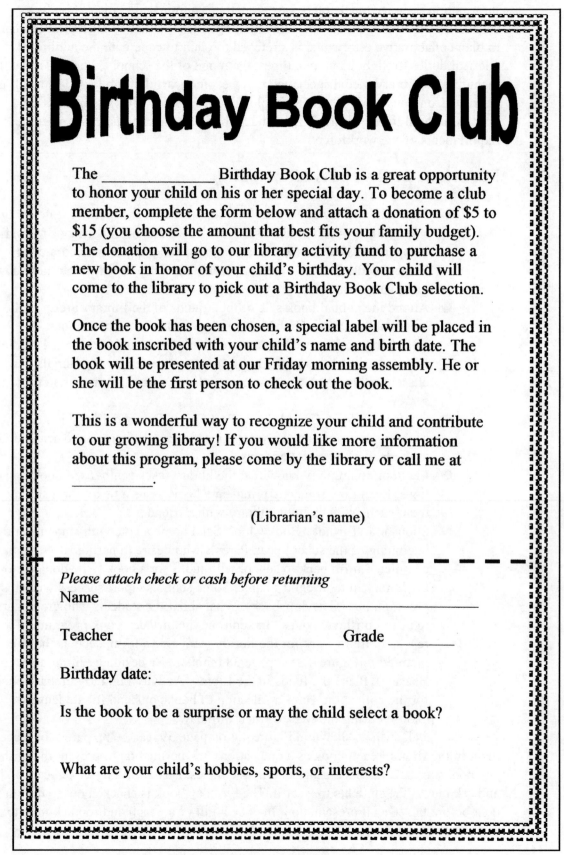

Birthday Book Club

The _____ Birthday Book Club is a great opportunity to honor your child on his or her special day. To become a club member, complete the form below and attach a donation of $5 to $15 (you choose the amount that best fits your family budget). The donation will go to our library activity fund to purchase a new book in honor of your child's birthday. Your child will come to the library to pick out a Birthday Book Club selection.

Once the book has been chosen, a special label will be placed in the book inscribed with your child's name and birth date. The book will be presented at our Friday morning assembly. He or she will be the first person to check out the book.

This is a wonderful way to recognize your child and contribute to our growing library! If you would like more information about this program, please come by the library or call me at _____.

(Librarian's name)

Please attach check or cash before returning

Name _____

Teacher _____Grade _____

Birthday date: _____

Is the book to be a surprise or may the child select a book?

What are your child's hobbies, sports, or interests?

Supplies

Place a recycle box in the teacher workroom to garner any unused bulletin board materials or supplies. Use discarded paper as notepad material for students to write call numbers. To save paper, use office stamps. Order stamps that state "Overdue" and "Lost." Stamp the word onto the sheet of paper your automation system generates, and sign "Thank you" and your name, thus eliminating a separate letter to parents.

When ordering supplies, use sale catalogs. Many library supply companies often offer discounts in the summer. You can find good deals on office supplies when "Back to School" sales begin in August. Order similar supplies at the same time to get a volume discount. Look for companies that offer free shipping. Find vendors at conventions that offer free library and office supplies, as well as decorative posters.

A Final Note

A difficult economy can create problems for school funding, which trickle down to library funding. The library media specialist who accepts the challenge uses creativity to overcome the problem. Search far and wide for other resources to fund the library program. Never become complacent in hard times. Speak out for the students because they are the ones who are most affected by loss of library funds.

Figure 4.4: Birthday Book Club Dedication Label

This book has been donated by Birthday Book Club Member

_____
(Name)

(Month, day, current year)

Chapter 5

Grant My Wish

Grants can be a great avenue for additional funding for many areas in the library media center. Grants provide much-needed equipment, materials, and supplies from public and private corporations and foundations. Writing a grant requires knowing the techniques to make it successful.

The Key to Grant Writing Success

Organization Identity

In his seminars, grant writer Kenneth Witherspoon uses a simple exercise to help grant writers think about their organizations. The exercise begins with basic thoughts about the school library media center and graduates to encompass its full scope of existence. Try the following exercise over a one- or two-week period. The result is a more focused description of the library media center and its goals.

1. List five words that describe your library.
2. List five words that an outsider might use to describe the proposed project or library.
3. Give three "action words" to characterize the project or the library.
4. Write a sentence describing your library, the project, and the benefits expected upon completion.
5. Write a 25-word description of your library.
6. Write a five-year plan.

Where to Find Grants

The Foundation Center has a wonderful Web site <http://www.fdncenter.org/> with grant announcements and information on how to apply for grants from private foundations. Included in the site is *The Proposal Writing Short Course*

<http://www.fdncenter.org/learn/shortcourse/prop1.html>, where the novice writer can find many tips about writing grants.

Foundation directories and grant indexes can be found in The Foundation Center's cooperating collections in all 50 states of the United States, as well as in its own libraries in Atlanta, Cleveland, New York, San Francisco, and Washington, DC. The Foundation Center also offers a Foundation Directory Online version at a subscriber cost. The Foundation libraries and cooperating collections serve as a bridge between nonprofit organizations and foundations that provide grants. Some cooperating collection libraries offer proposal reviews and recommendations by staff members. Information from federal and state agencies can lead the library media specialist to more opportunities for funding. Local community organizations and businesses also sponsor funding for schools.

The American Library Association (ALA) Web site includes a list of grant writing opportunities at< http://www.ala.org/>. The American Association of School Libraries <http://www.ala.org/aasl/awards.html>, a division of the American Library Association, also includes grant opportunities.

Network with fellow grant writers. Many large cities have meetings where grant writers, both professional and novice, meet to share ideas and current grant announcements.

Choosing the Right Grant

Perform a needs assessment. This step is perhaps the most critical. Create a committee of parents, faculty, fellow library media specialists, or members of your Library Advisory Committee. The committee determines the methods of assessment. Existing school data, questionnaires, interviews, and focus groups provide the necessary information about the school's current needs.

Next, examine the school and community data, and set priorities. Provide answers to the following questions:

1. What are the needs of the library media center and the school?
2. Which needs are long-term, and which are short-term?
3. How do the needs of the library media center mesh with those of the school? Do they have a common thread?
4. Which of the library's needs will be addressed first?

Compare the school needs with the mission and goals of various funding organizations. Research foundations that enable the school library media center to address specific campus needs and problems.

Writing a Letter of Inquiry

Many times, a foundation or corporation has specific instructions about the content of the letter of inquiry. Obey the guidelines, and the chance of rejection is minimized. Most letters of inquiry contain the following instructions about what to include:

- State the project clearly. If the project has a title, make sure it encompasses every aspect of it.
- Briefly outline activities and outcomes.
- Connect the goals of the library media center to those of the foundation or corporation.
- Clearly describe the community your school serves. Note any important demographic or geographic points.
- "Tell," not "sell." The inquiry letter should put the focus upon the project, not why your library media center is deserving of the funding.
- Watch the attitude of the letter. Do not slant the letter toward either extreme of excessive need or righteous worthiness of the monetary reward of funding.

Writing a Winning Proposal

Basic Tips

- Remember that neatness and clarity do count.
- Keep it brief.
- Be positive.
- Be careful with assumptions. Explain who is applying for the grant, and show evidence of cause and effect.
- Always ask someone who is not connected with education to review the proposal. Can the reviewer clearly see what the program is and what it needs? Often, a profession's special language creeps into the wording. Foundations or corporations may not be familiar with terms used in the education field.

The Parts of a Proposal

1. **Program Objectives** Objectives must be concrete and measurable. Do not confuse objectives with goals. The program objectives section should state who, what, when, how much, and how the program will be measured.
2. **Methods Used** This section contains the activities and names of the personnel who carry out the program objectives. List the management plans for securing data, the use of resources, training requirements, and facilities.
3. **Evaluation Plan** This section explains how the achievement of objectives will be measured. The evaluation can be expressed in quantitative or qualitative data. Quantitative data is numerically based. It describes a percentage of students or other measures to achieve the program goal. Qualitative data is the result of observing the progress of the program and expressing in a narrative manner.
4. **Continuation Plan** This is the place to answer the questions: How will the project continue beyond the funding period provided by the grant? Will the program become fee-based? Will the campus budget allocate additional funds? Will new grant sources be explored?
5. **The Budget** Be as specific as possible. Predicting the cost of materials when the grant is awarded is difficult at times. Note both personnel and nonpersonnel expenditures.
6. **The Appendix** Place any requested or required support materials in the appendix. Materials may include an IRS Nonprofit Determination Letter, names and qualifications of project administrators, and letters of support that the foundation or corporation requests. Do not send letters of support unless directly instructed to do so by the funder.

A Final Checklist

Great proposals:

- Focus on the library media center and school's needs
- Reflect the funder's interests and focus
- Are based upon a review of the funder's previous grant awards to other schools
- Are brief (ten pages, maximum; five is an ideal length without attachments)
- Creatively address a problem
- Clearly define the program
- Demonstrate how the funding will directly impact the student population
- Include plans for the continuance of the program
- Include all the attachments required

Gruesome proposals:

- Fail to demonstrate the need for the program
- Try to fit the proposal into a grant intended for only specific populations
- Use terms unfamiliar to the funder
- Reflect a crisis or unplanned need
- Include materials not requested by the funder, such as letters of support
- Misrepresent the school by withholding information
- Are long
- Contain budgets that are unrealistic and vague

The Waiting

Once the grant is completed and sent off, the waiting begins. Remember that the review process by the foundation or corporation is sometimes lengthy. At this time, think about how the school and the library media center will accept the funding or deal with rejection of the proposal. If the grant is awarded, be sure to say "Thank you" in a written format. The importance of being thankful cannot be overstated. Foundations and corporations are made up of people, and this simple oversight can harm the relationship in future grant requests. Quickly send any required reports to the funder. Rejection is difficult, especially because writing a grant is time-consuming. Contact the organization to inquire about the reason for rejection. Writing a successful grant is a learning experience. Read grants that have been awarded as clues to what could be included in future grant applications. Finally, try and try again.

Chapter 6

Programs to Motivate a Student to Read

The Goal

Creating lifelong learners is a goal for all educators, especially the library media specialist. Instilling the desire to read is a complicated task. Many variables must be present to fulfill the goal:

- Students must be motivated.
- Material must be of interest to the student population.
- Reading levels of material must be appropriate for student success.

This chapter is devoted to examining several reading motivation programs. Each program is introduced in an easy-to-follow format. A promotion plan, supply list, forms, and directions accompany each program.

Supervision

To be successful, a reading program needs to be closely supervised. The majority of the reading for the program occurs in the classroom or at home. A line is placed on each reading program progress chart for a signature. Send a note home to parents with the progress chart attached. Involving parents with the reading program is an important component of its success. Be sure to tell students that books can be found at the school library, public library, and bookstore to read for the program. Some reading programs count books read by teachers to the whole class.

Rewards

Most reading motivation programs involve a reward upon the completion of a task. Whenever possible, try to keep the rewards as closely related to reading and writing as possible, such as bookmarks, pencils, pens, erasers, and paperbacks. Toys and trinkets do not reinforce your goal: a love of reading and lifelong learning. Parties including food are strong motivators. However, try to make sure a book discussion guides some of the conversation at the party.

Reading Motivation Programs

Many states have lists of books on a recommended list for students in public school. For example, the list in Texas for elementary students is "The Texas Bluebonnet Reading List." The following ideas would work just as well with any state reading program:

Grade Level: 3–5

Promotion Plan: Begin the reading program by booktalking or reading selections to students. Make posters of the reading list, and give them to the teachers to post in the classroom. Some of the materials from the state library may have a chart or graph upon which each class can plot the number of books read. A minimum number of books is required in order to be eligible to vote. To stimulate interest beyond the required number, offer additional rewards at various increments of books read. For example:

- Five: Name on poster in library
- Ten: Bookmark and a pencil
- Fifteen: Journal and a pen
- Twenty: A button that says "State Reading Expert" and an invitation to the State Book Club Brunch in the library. During brunch, students discuss their favorite books.

Supplies:

- Craft paper, assorted colors
- Scissors
- Construction paper
- Double-sided tape
- Dry erase or permanent marker

Directions:

1. Laminate 9 by 12 inch white or pale colored construction paper.
2. Construct a large poster from craft paper of one of the state's symbols. Laminate it and attach it to a wall in the library media center.

3. Using scissors (or a die-cut machine), cut laminated construction paper into the shape of the state.
4. When students have read the required number of books to be eligible to vote for their favorite, write their names in marker on the state shape, and tape to the giant poster in the library.

Connecting with the Public Library

Public librarians appreciate as many connections as possible with the school library. School library media specialists promote summer reading programs, such as the following example, during the last few months of the school year. Reinforce summer reading by offering rewards in the following school year.

Reading + Summer = Fun

Grade Level: K–5

Promotion Plan: This simple reading program rewards the students who accomplish reading goals, whether in minutes or number of books read. Students keep track of their progress during the summer and bring their form to the library media specialist when school begins. The library media specialist issues a coupon in the form of a discount on any one item in the first book fair of the school year (see the coupon in Figure 6.1 for an example). Use $1 to $2 as an amount for the coupons. Keep a running record of these coupons when used at the book fair, and adjust the percentage of profit in free books.

Figure 6.1: Reward Coupon for Book Fair Promotion

Adapting Sports

Sports games have incremental goals and are highly adaptable to reading programs. Sports related reading programs also can be used to spark interest in existing computerized reading management programs, such as *Reading Counts*™ and *Accelerated Reader*™.

The following programs can be adapted to a variety of sports for all students.

Be a Reading Hero (Football, Soccer, Swimming)

Grade Level: 3–5

Promotion Plan: Use the reading hero program to help students discover the Dewey Decimal Classification System. Students read two (or more) books per decimal

Figure 6.2: Progress Chart Using Football Hero Motif

Be a Reading Hero

Student Name _____ Grade ____ Teacher _____
Signature: _____

000-299	Title _____
	Title _____
300-399	Title _____
	Title _____
400-499	Title _____
	Title _____
500-599	Title _____
	Title _____
699-699	Title _____
	Title _____
700-799	Title _____
	Title _____
800-899	Title _____
	Title _____
900-999	Title _____
	Title _____

TOUCHDOWN!!

classification. Due to the possible drain on some sections of the nonfiction area, you may wish to start classes in different numbers.

Supplies:

- Progress chart (Figure 6.2)
- Pencil

Directions:

1. The students chart progress by coloring or shading in the yardage on the progress chart. The students also list the titles of the books they have read.
2. The culmination of the program is a hero sandwich party. At the party, ask students to discuss their favorite Dewey decimal categories and booktalk a title they found interesting.

Books Are a Hit!

Grade Level: K–5

Promotion Plan: Use the sport of baseball to tally the total minutes students read. For example:

- First Base = 150 minutes
- Second Base = 300 minutes
- Third Base = 450 minutes
- Home Run = 600 minutes

Supplies:

- Progress chart (Figure 6.3 on page 52)
- Pencil

Directions:

1. Students log the number of minutes read at each session. Homework does not count. Reading assignments do count. Students can include material from magazines and newspapers.
2. When each goal has been achieved, students shade or color in the appropriate base and receive a sticker to place on their chart.
3. When all bases are colored in, students receive a larger award, certificate, or party.

Figure 6.3: Progress Chart Using Baseball Motif

Name _____ Grade _____ Teacher _____

BOOKS ARE A HIT!

<u>Directions:</u> Log in the day and number of minutes you have read on the chart below. Be sure an adult signs the form. If you need more room, attach a sheet of notebook paper. When you have reached the amount of minutes by each base, color the base and turn this form into the library.

Date	Minutes	Signature	Date	Minutes	Signature

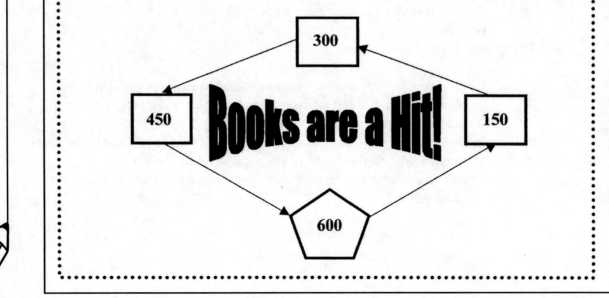

Using the School Mascot

Use the school mascot as a model for a reading motivation program. Following is an example from a school with dinosaurs as the mascot:

Dinosaurs Dig Reading

Grade Level: 3–5

Promotion Plan: The aim of the program is to promote reading in different genres of fiction: realistic fiction, historical fiction, fantasy, and mysteries. However, this program can be easily adapted into a reading minutes accumulation program for the entire school. The program also works well when introducing or reinforcing the Dewey Decimal Classification System. The reward is a Volcano Ice Cream Party for successful participants.

Supplies:

- Dinosaur Chart Strip (Figure 6.4)
- Colored pencils and markers
- Notebook paper or chart
- Volcano Ice Cream Sculpture:
  - ▲ ice cream (three gallons, or more for larger crowds)
  - ▲ chocolate syrup (buy extra to put more on student servings)
  - ▲ Maraschino cherries
  - ▲ whipped cream
  - ▲ candy or cookie dinosaur shapes
  - ▲ large aluminum roasting pan
  - ▲ large spoons
  - ▲ plastic spoons and bowls for students

Directions:

1. Spend 30 to 45 minutes discussing the different genres in the fiction section.

Figure 6.4: Dinosaur Chart Strip

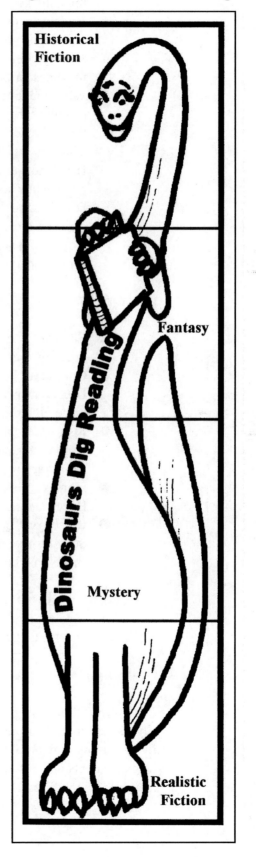

2. Show students how reading a book jacket or cover can help them to determine the genre.
3. Students read two selections from each genre and record the title and an adult signature on the sheet of notebook paper.
4. As they complete the genre, students color in the corresponding section on the dinosaur bookmark.
5. When the form is completed, write the student's name on a dinosaur shape, and place the shape on a bulletin board prepared for the reading program.
6. Reward students with the Volcano Ice Cream Party. Make sure you have adults to help assemble the ice cream volcano and manage the students. Here's how to assemble the volcano:

Slightly soften the ice cream, and mound into the metal roasting pan. Drizzle chocolate syrup like lava from the top of the volcano. Squirt whipped cream (smoke) on top. Add the cherry. Place cookie dinosaurs on the volcano slopes. Be sure to take photographs of the volcano and the students enjoying the fun.

More Ideas

- **Eagles** "The Eagles Soar into Reading"
  Students record their goals onto bird shapes to place on a bulletin board.
- **Cougars, Tigers, Bears, or Lions** "Paws and Read a While"
  Use a paw print pattern for students to record progress. Laminate and place on the floor and walls of the library media center.
- **Fish** "Get into the Swim of Reading"
  Use fish shapes and beach party themes to decorate a bulletin board and the library media center.
- **Horses** "Gallop into Reading"
  Have students record progress onto horseshoe shapes.
- **Cowboys** "Lasso a Good Book"
  Students record their reading progress on book shapes. Place the book shape on a bulletin board with a rope around the edges.

Programs with Special Interest

Take a Culture Cruise

Grade Level: 2–6

Promotion Plan: The goal of this reading program is to promote the cultural diversity of the school learning community. The program familiarizes students with different regions and people of the world. The event is an excellent way to enlist the help of parents and volunteers from other countries. Students select fiction books that are set in a different country or nonfiction about another country.

Supplies:

- Paper passport (Figure 6.5 on page 56)
- Color copier paper
- Rubber stamp

Directions:

1. Share with students that they will be taking an around-the-world cruise via books.
2. Have students select 10 countries to visit. Books can be fiction or non-fiction. The fiction books must be set in a foreign location.
3. Give students a copy of the passport for the journey (Figure 6.5). Print the form on the front and back of one sheet of paper. Ask students to fold the passport down the dotted lines. After selecting the book, the students write the country visited on the reading record form.
4. When students have completed a book, the library staff or library media specialist stamps the passport. An adult or parent signature is required.
5. Reward the students with a Culture Cruise Party. Decorate the library media center like a cruise ship with posters of foreign ports of call on the walls. Enlist the help of parents or volunteers who are from other countries to prepare their favorite food.

Readers Are Leaders

Grade Level: 4–6

Promotion Plan: The goal of this program is to acquaint students with famous people. Collaborate with teachers to determine when to begin the reading program. Many teachers emphasize biographies in January and February of the school year.

Supplies:

- Pencil
- Paper

Directions:

1. Have students read biographies of five to ten famous people, depending upon the time length of the reading program.
2. Reward students with a button that says "Read to Lead." Students dress up in costume and create a video of famous sayings or accomplishments of each famous person.

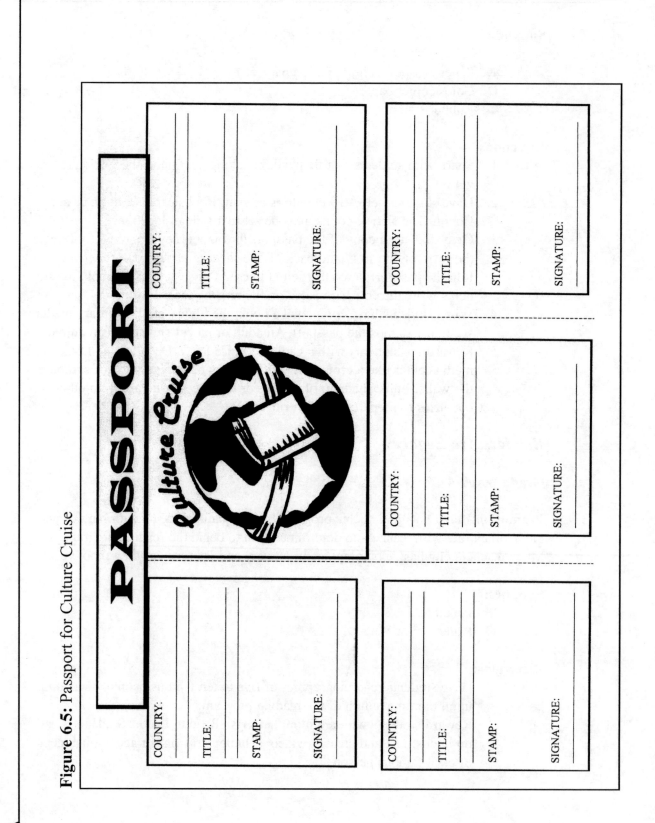

Figure 6.5: Passport for Culture Cruise

One-Night Events

Storytelling Festival

Storytelling Festivals are a great way to involve the entire learning community. Begin by presenting storytelling sessions to students. Fourth and fifth grade students make excellent storytellers. Ask teachers to recommend one or two students per class to learn the craft of storytelling. Students choose a folktale or a story to retell in their own words. Practice weekly so students feel comfortable telling a story. Create a name for your company of student storytellers, such as (School Name) Storytelling Troupe. Many teachers are excellent storytellers. Contact a local storytelling guild for more adult storytellers. Place three storytellers in each classroom. Be sure to place an adult storyteller or chaperone in classrooms of student storytellers. Adults help monitor time and behavior. Students and parents choose a room they would like to visit. Here is a sample schedule:

Figure 6.6: Schedule for Storytelling Festival

Time	Room Number 101	Room Number 102
7:00–7:30	Teacher Storyteller	Adult Storyteller
7:30–8:00	Student Storyteller	Student Storyteller
8:00–8:30	Student Storyteller	Student Storyteller

Family Reading Fun

Enlist teachers and community volunteers to read their favorite stories to the students. If the program is held at night, students can come dressed in pajamas. Ideas for volunteer readers include local high school athletic teams, teachers, district administrators, local professional sports teams, and public librarians. While the students are in rooms being read to, parents meet to learn more about reading to children. Bring in district experts and public librarians for a panel discussion. Leave time for a question and answer period.

　　　With some time, the library media specialist can stimulate reading interest with reading motivation programs. The result is always positive. Students have fun, plus their reading ability and confidence rises.

Chapter 7

The Library Media Specialist as Collaborator and Reading Advocate

The Curriculum Collaborator Role

School districts are aligning curriculum to statewide teaching standards. Library media specialists who have ideas that directly relate to the classroom curriculum and standards are worth their weight in gold. Teachers gain new respect for the library media specialist who seeks them out and offers to lend a helping hand.

Instructing students in library research skills in isolation from a topic is futile. Only when information and need are combined are library skills relevant. Many of the ideas in this chapter incorporate activities in which the teacher and the library media specialist can collaborate on pre-writing activities, curriculum objectives, and information skills.

A central finding of The Second Colorado Study, *How School Librarians Help Kids Achieve Standards* (2000), shows the importance of adopting a collaborative method to improve information literacy. The study reported that test scores rose in elementary schools where library media specialists and teachers worked together to achieve learning goals. When the library media specialist provided in-service training for teachers about new methods to access information, test scores also increased.

What Is Collaboration?

Collaborating with a teacher is more than locating books for units or instructing a class on the technique of taking notes. Collaboration involves face-to-face planning with a teacher in the building. Both partners in education determine the objectives to be achieved based on content standards, compose instructional steps in the unit, and share in the evaluation process of the unit.

How to Start the Process

Talk to the Principal

Without administrative support, collaboration efforts will be minimal. Show the principal the charts published in The Second Colorado Study. Test scores are the measure by which schools are awarded recognition, so a receptive mind is already in place. Emphasize how administrative support in word and deed is crucial. Note the level of commitment that is extended. A lukewarm response means more effort on the part of the library media specialist and less result in collaboration events.

Listen to Teachers

Eat lunch in the teacher's lounge, and notice any difficulties teachers discuss. If they frequently mention the lack of time to teach core subjects, speak up. Do not try to convince the teachers to collaborate with you — show them how you can make their life easier. Be the support person that they need. Emphasize that two teachers are better than one. Keep the discussion relaxed and friendly. Offering to help teach any technology applications in the project can pull reluctant collaborators into the ring. Host a lunch in the library that expands all of the teachers' lunchtime schedules. Display new books and a notebook featuring successful collaboration efforts. Include many rubrics used in note taking and data gathering. Any comments by the teacher can lead to an explanation of the project. A new collaboration partner is in sight! Ask the new teachers if they need help. They are usually overwhelmed and grateful for any help.

Model the Process

Teachers may not know what collaboration with the library media specialist looks like in action. Collaboration with the library media specialist is not taught in the undergraduate education department. Collaboration — a big word that sounds like more work, teachers think. Show how the process can help ease instruction and evaluation time. Demonstrate the collaboration process with a PowerPoint presentation at a faculty meeting. Two things might happen: offers from teachers and an impressed principal.

Be Prepared

Find out the subjects that are studied at each grade level. Send a sheet of paper or an e-mail message, or casually ask teachers at the beginning of the year about the subjects covered during the year and the timetable. When it is time to visit the grade level, the library media specialist comes prepared with resources, such as reference sources, Web sites, ideas for teaching information skills, and a sample lesson. Offer creative project suggestions:

- Make a bag to hold important information about the project, and tell about each item.
- Make up a song about the project.
- Publish a brochure on the subject, state, or country that was assigned.
- Assist the students in the creation of a Web site or PowerPoint presentation about their project.
- Show how databases and spreadsheets can display information.

Do Not Drown Teachers in Paper

Try not to overwhelm your prospective collaboration partner. Requiring the teacher to do extra paper work and submit copies of lesson plans can create a negative response. Keep the collaboration plan to one page, such as the example in Figure 7.1 on page 62. Both parties keep a copy of the plan, and activities are clearly laid out.

After a project is completed with a teacher, put it on display in the library media center. When people ask about the project, emphasize which teacher worked collaboratively and how positive the experience was for all. Publicity pays in more collaboration with reluctant teachers.

A Sample Collaboration Unit

Teacher Name(s): Ms. Right, second grade teacher
Date of the Project: January
Subject: Penguins
Content Area Standards: CONTENT STANDARD C: Life Science: Penguins

- The characteristics of penguins
- Life cycles of penguins
- Penguins and their environment

The National Science Education Standards are available at <http://books.nap.edu/html/nses/html/index.html>.

What Are the Information Literacy Standards Addressed in the Project/Unit?

The Information Literacy Standards created by the American Library Association can be found at <http://www.ala.org/aasl/ip_nine.html>. Standards one, two, three, and nine are addressed in this collaboration unit. (See Appendix F, page 104.)

What Role Does Each Collaboration Partner Play?

The teacher:

- Instructs students about the habitats, body characteristics, and distinguishing features of different types of penguins
- Assigns groups of students to research a penguin type
- Works with the library media specialist to create a rubric for students to record information

Figure 7.1: Collaboration Planning Form

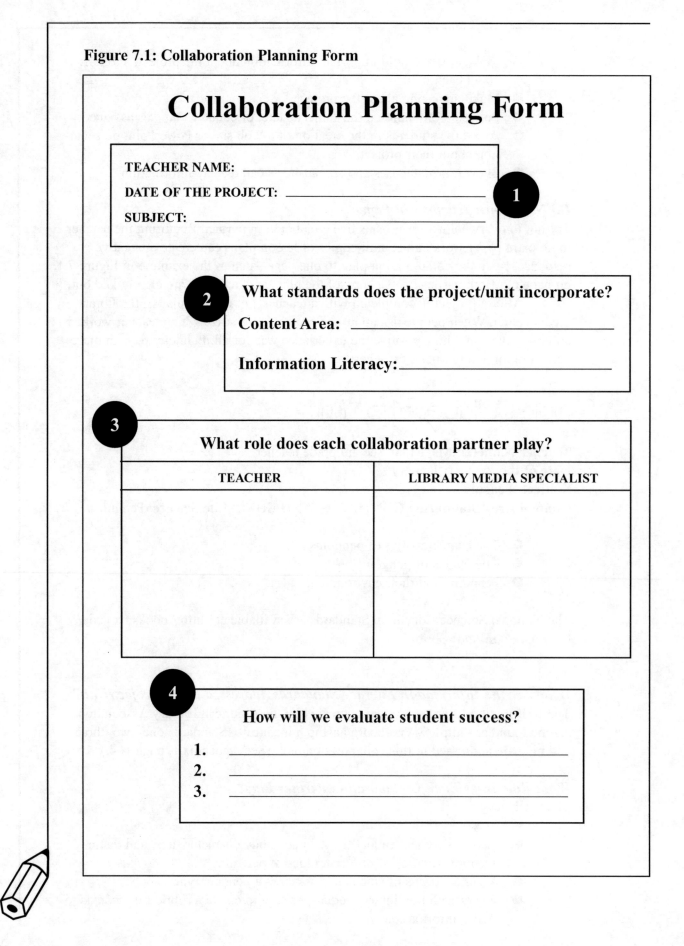

Collaboration Planning Form

TEACHER NAME: _____

DATE OF THE PROJECT: _____   **1**

SUBJECT: _____

2   What standards does the project/unit incorporate?

Content Area: _____

Information Literacy: _____

3   What role does each collaboration partner play?

TEACHER	LIBRARY MEDIA SPECIALIST

4   How will we evaluate student success?

1. _____
2. _____
3. _____

The librarian:

- Gathers information on penguin types from many sources, such as Web sites, databases, books, online encyclopedias, and magazines
- Instructs students how to begin a simple research process, such as questions that need to be asked about penguins, where to find information, and how to use information
- Uses a rubric that helps students record information about their penguin type
- Assists groups of students with the creation of a PowerPoint presentation about the penguin type

How Will the Collaboration Partners Evaluate Student Success?

- Did the student groups use accurate information?
- Was the presentation clear and understandable?
- Was the presentation creative in its approach of the subject?

The Reading Advocate Role

Playing a part in the students' desire to know more about a subject and promoting the joy of reading are two of the most important parts of the library media specialist's job. Library media specialists assist in reading instruction and ardently promote reading at every turn. Inspiring students to read takes a great deal of thought and planning. Try the following ideas to keep students reading:

1. Form a lunchtime book club to discuss the plot, characterization, setting, dialogue, and so on of a book.
2. Instead of booktalking, dramatize a section of the book.
3. Create a new book jacket for a book, depicting the type of book as well as the story line.
4. Ask the students to guess what the story is about from the new jacket.
5. Have students act out the story after reading it.
6. Ask students to write a class poem after the story is read.
7. Direct students to write a different ending to the book.
8. Have students pantomime an action in the book.
9. If the story or book has geographical information, find a large wall map and locate the area.
10. Encourage different students to pick a few of their favorite books. Create a "(Name's) Picks of the Week" area on a table or shelf in the library media center.

What about the student "who can't find anything good to read" in the library media center? Reluctant reader is the term usually used for such students. When the library media specialist searches resources for reading material, the result is a list of books for students who are in higher grades. Subject matter and reading level are often not appropriate for the young reader. In the elementary school, reading ability and reading attitude combine to create problems in book selection. Students having difficulty reading tend to grow more hesitant to read for pleasure as they progress through school. Peer pressure in the elementary classroom may further complicate the matter. The avid readers in the classroom are tackling thicker books, while the struggling reader, to save face, attempts the same material. Frustration is usually the result. The following material may inspire struggling readers in levels two to three:

- *Magic Treehouse* series by Mary Pope Osborne
- *Cam Jansen* series by David Adler
- *Bailey School Kids Adventures* by Debbie Dadey and Marcia Thornton Jones
- *A to Z Mysteries* by Ron Roy
- Sports titles by Matt Christopher
- *Kids of Polk Street School* series by Patricia Reilly Giff
- *Junie B. Jones* series by Barbara Park
- *Marvin K. Redpost* series by Louis Sachar
- *Nate the Great* series by Marjorie Weinman Sharmat
- *Encyclopedia Brown* series by Donald J. Sobol
- *Julian* series by Ann Cameron
- *Berenstain Bears* chapter books by Stan and Jan Berenstain
- *Arthur* chapter books by Marc Brown
- *Herbie Jones* series by Suzy Kline

Many students prefer paperback books. Paperbacks are cheap and plentiful. Often, some titles are not available in hardcover, but are in paperback versions. The library media specialist can receive a percentage of free books in paperback from a book fair to begin the collection. Use a laminated cover to extend the life of titles that are favorites among the students. Write the first letter of the author's last name on the spine, and place the book on a cart or in a basket in the fiction or nonfiction area. The use of the letter makes it easier to locate the book later.

To encourage boys to read, author Jon Scieszka has created a reading program called "Guys Read!" The Web site <http://www.guysread.com> contains a reading list for all ages, a mission statement, and advice for bookstores, teachers, librarians, and guys. Scieszka suggests that librarians look at the library's collection from a boy's point of view and ask if he would find it interesting. Another suggestion is to form a father-son or parent-son book club.

Library media specialists are information managers as well as promoters of the lifelong habit of reading. No other person in the school environment has access to all students to promote student literacy. Captivating and inspiring the imaginations of young minds is perhaps one of the most enjoyable parts of working in a library media center.

Chapter 8

Encouraging Staff to Use New Technology

Technology has changed education. Years ago, subject matter was introduced, taught, and tested by a single source, the teacher. Textbooks were used to augment the teacher's instruction. The student delivered a product that used only one medium: paper. Today, many sources of information are available to students in a variety of formats. Library media specialists, teachers, and students collaborate on the information received, and plan the product and method of evaluation. In many cases, the student's final product is now multimedia-based.

Times have changed, and some teachers are challenged to become the facilitators of more technology than they are comfortable with. Fear of failure and the lack of confidence keep many library media specialists and teachers from venturing forward. However, there is good news: library media specialists and teachers do not need to become technology experts! In today's classroom and library media center, everyone learns together and gives up some of the direct lesson control. The classroom teacher presents students with real problems to investigate. These problems reflect the students' issues faced in their homes and communities, as well as in their future workplaces. The students brainstorm solutions, summarize results in groups, and seek resolutions from material gathered in a self-guided manner. Everyone in the classroom collaborates to internalize and to enjoy learning. The process occurs over several weeks, transcends subject lines, and is supported by technology. The teacher assesses the learning process by observing and interviewing groups of students. The following scenario represents an example of this approach:

Example of Collaboration Using Technology

- The teacher describes the problem: the lack of biographical material on local multicultural heroes. Students brainstorm for a solution. The result: creating a set of videotapes and CDs, plus accompanying text.
- The students learn about the interview process. The library media specialist provides materials in book and video form of interviews with national figures. The local history museum provides materials and detailed information on community leaders.
- The students discover the content and type of questions (open-ended versus closed-ended questions) they would ask the interviewees. They learn about basic techniques, such as eye contact and posture.
- In groups, the students practice interviewing techniques. The group is formed with three students in each of the following roles: cameraperson, interviewer, and recorder. Each team analyzes its style in videotaped practice interviews.
- After the interview, the groups summarize the information from the videotaped session and the text of the recorder. They review their technique and offer one another suggestions.
- The teacher moves from group to group in the various stages of the project. He or she monitors student progress and suggests questions to explore.

Time is another hindrance in the use of technology tools in the library media center and classroom. Teachers wonder how they can fit another requirement into their daily schedule. Technology training takes time. Teachers and staff may not understand why they have to learn a new tool when the old ones worked just as well. Library media specialists and teachers are sometimes confused about when to use technology in instruction.

This chapter is dedicated to answering four questions that are important to the library media specialist and faculty:

1. What is technology?
2. Why use technology?
3. How can technology training be implemented in a timely and successful manner?
4. When should technology, such as hardware or software tools, be used in curriculum planning for a subject?

What Is Technology?

When people first see the word *technology*, they often think of computers and the Internet. Somehow, this limited concept has become ingrained in educators' thinking as districts continue to buy and upgrade computers and presentation software. The

Merriam-Webster OnLine Dictionary < http://www.m-w.com/home.htm> defines technology as "a manner of accomplishing a task especially using technical processes, methods, or knowledge." The true meaning of the term *technology* addresses not only the hardware and software, but also curriculum innovation. Even e-mail correspondence can be a technology tool when applied to a teacher's lesson plan. To completely understand the scope of technology, educators need to answer one simple question: "What media shall I use to maximize my students' learning?" Re-thinking technology tools results in freedom of choice for both educators and students.

Why Use Technology?

For the Students
One of the goals in education is to produce information-literate students. Information technology provides the tools to produce a student who can investigate, analyze, synthesize, and evaluate information for use. An information-literate student uses the technology tool to help solve a problem. Therefore, using technology should not be limited to drill and practice exercises. Thinking comes first; the quest for a solution is primary. Technology tools are of a secondary nature. Technology is the medium used to explore beyond the walls of the school. For example, when studying a foreign country, students can send a request for keypals to a mailing list via the IECC (Intercultural E-mail Classroom Connections) mailing list and learn first-hand about life in another part of the world. The Web site address for IECC is <http://www.teaching.com/iecc/>. The Web site serves over 7,000 teachers in 82 countries.

For the National Standards
The National Educational Technology Standards project (NETS), a project of the International Society for Technology in Education (ISTE), is creating benchmarks for K–12 campuses in an effort to improve technology education for all students. ISTE, or the International Society for Technology in Education <http://cnets.iste.org/> seeks out ways to integrate technology into the everyday curriculum and evaluate its usage. This site provides a listing of the technology standards for teachers and students of all grade levels. For elementary schools, the standards are broken into two categories: kindergarten through grade two, and grade three through grade five. Extensive lesson plans for grade levels are available. Each lesson indicates which NETS Performance Indicators have been met by each section of the activity. The resources and activities can be found in the publication *NETS for Students: Connecting Curriculum and Technology*.

For Professional and Personal Enrichment
"Why should I use technology?" teachers ask. Why would a teacher with every minute of the day mapped out take time to learn about using Webcasts in the classroom? Why would a seasoned veteran abandon years of tried and true instructional techniques to learn Web page design so the class can launch a Web page based upon a subject matter? Sure, the district supervisor may require technology expertise, and standards will have to be met, but what does it take to inspire a teacher to catch a

vision of the future? If the library media specialist can answer these questions, teachers just might sign up for the technology journey. Technology facilitator Henry Vasquez calls it the "light bulb effect." Inspiration comes as the result of demonstrating a timesaving shortcut to a teacher, finding an innovative lesson plan using the Internet, or many other serendipitous moments. Before long, the teacher utters those profound words, "I want to try this."

How to Use Technology: Valued Training

The Principal: The First Point of Contact

Without the principal's support, a school-wide technology focus is difficult to obtain. Primarily, administrators need to be shown how technology can save time and deliver direct, clear results. Student achievement is the benchmark of a successful school. The library media specialist's job is to show how information technology tools support the achievement of the information-literate student. To enlist a principal's support, try using the following tips:

- Use spreadsheets and charts in your correspondence with the principal.
- Ask to show a PowerPoint presentation to the faculty outlining the technology available on the campus.
- Demonstrate the media tools at faculty meetings.
- Invite the principal to attend a technology conference.
- Present research, such as the Second Colorado Study *How School Librarians Help Kids Achieve Standards* (2000). This study supports evidence for the link between higher reading test scores and the availability of information technology for students. For more details, see Chapter 4.

Training the Staff

Training in technology takes time. Teachers have tremendous time pressures in their daily schedule. They also are more apt to be comfortable with what has worked in the past. To save time and stress, use some of the following ideas:

Assess Previous Technology Experience

Find out how comfortable the faculty is with technology. Assess the teachers' technology skills by asking what hardware or software they are familiar with. Be sure to stress that teachers do not need to become technology experts.

Make Training Relevant: The Need to Know

Provide staff development seminars that deal directly with everyday issues. Technology instruction for staff development is not limited to instruction on the use of random types of software. Exceptional technology staff development determines the needs in the classroom. What hardware or software can positively impact the students' learning? Good technology training develops ideas and generates practical solutions and presentation methods. When instruction in using a piece of software is matched with a teacher's curriculum objective, true learning takes place.

Take It Slow

Proceed slowly. Most people who are new to the world of technology are afraid of failure. They may be afraid of what others will think of their level of technology expertise. Therefore, praise teachers and staff often as they gain new levels of expertise.

Watch the Attitude

Success for a reluctant staff depends upon the library media specialist's attitude while training others. Disdain for the staff's efforts and progress can block learning. Resistance to technology can occur. Be patient, and do not try to demand a higher level of progress than is realistic. Be available for questions and re-teaching. Becoming familiar with different media and presentation methods takes a great deal of repetition. People cannot remember how to perform a task they were shown months ago. Prepare a "quick step" chart or paper bookmark for the staff and faculty to aid the memory.

Provide a Mentor

If some teachers learn quickly and are kind, patient souls, enlist them as mentors on the campus. Some successful schools have trained one person at each grade level to be the technology mentor. Be available to offer assistance and answer the questions of novice technology users. An impatient attitude can undo months of progress.

Hold Tech Chats

Many questions of new users are repetitious. To save time for all parties, offer a time to discuss problems and creative ideas. Pick one day a week after school for a quick gathering of interested staff members, and make the discussion session available as an e-mail to all faculty and staff. Post solutions and information on current technology innovations and collaboration ideas on the school Web page. Ask to be placed on the agenda of faculty meetings to inform all staff of the tech chats.

Go Online

Demonstrate online curriculum Web sites to the faculty. The more teachers venture online to solve their own lesson plan needs, the greater the use of technology solutions for the classroom. In addition, the teacher begins to feel comfortable and eager to pursue more training.

When to Use Technology

Making It Real

Many questions need to be answered when deciding how to use the appropriate information technology effectively. These questions are used as a litmus test separately or exclusively of one another.

- Does it translate to real-world experiences?
- Does it give emphasis to higher level thinking skills?
- Does it create audience excitement and interest about a subject or topic?
- Does it save time?

Figure 8.1a: Slides for Research Lesson

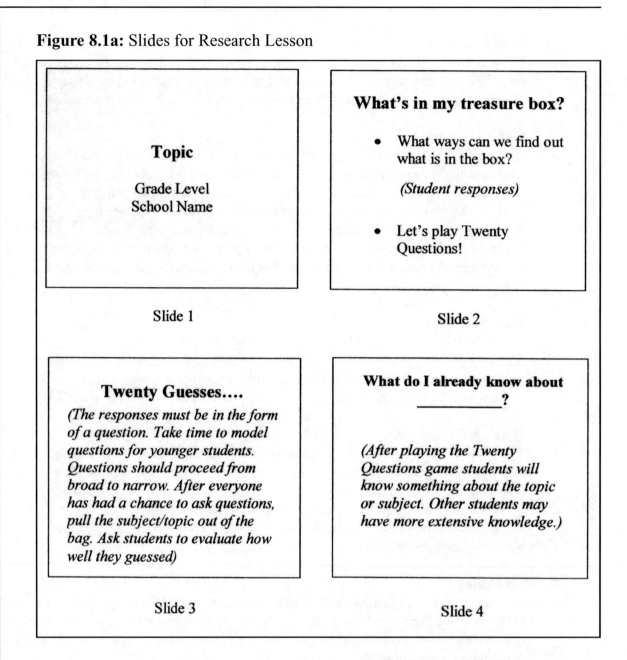

At the basic level, projects use keywords such as define, read, describe, review, apply, interpret, solve, compare, contrast, experiment, or explain. The library media specialist at this step can model the research process, provide materials, and optimize access for students. A sample presentation for modeling the research process is the PowerPoint example in Figure 8.1. This example is best used for first through third grade. Find a shoebox, and decorate it with craft ribbon and sequins for a treasure box. Place the object, such as an animal, into the treasure box. (Note: The remarks in italics and parentheses are for library media specialists and should not be included in the final slide preparation.)

At the next level, true collaboration can occur. These research projects synthesize the knowledge gathered. The library media specialist provides assistance with data collection, presentation, and evaluation whether hardware or software applications are used. This level of projects uses words such as judge, assess,

Figure 8.1b: Slides for Research Lesson

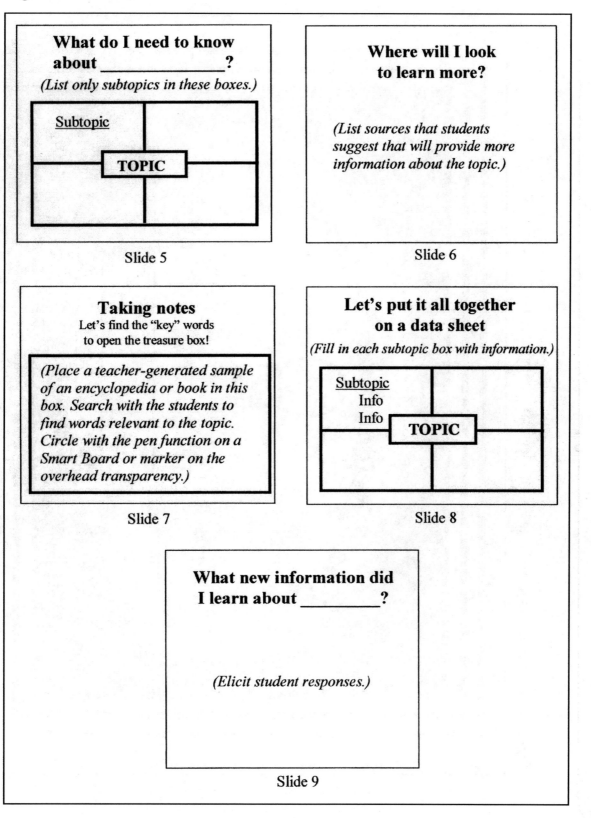

Figure 8.2: Recognition Certificate

compare, select, appraise, and evaluate. The library media specialist assists in the construction of the evaluation model.

Conducting a Trial Run

Before the teacher or library media specialist orchestrates a unit using technology applications or hardware, perform a trial run. Find answers to basic questions during this time, such as "How much time does the library media specialist need in the introduction of the research process?" "Will small groups be used?" "How will the small groups report?" "How long is the format of the final project?" "Are all parties comfortable with the presentation technology tools?" "Is everyone prepared for plan B should the technology equipment or application fail?"

Enticements for Reluctant Faculty

Sometimes the school faculty needs to be encouraged to begin using technology in the curriculum. The following ideas might motivate staff:

- Offer a prize for the best student research project. Stress innovative reports using multimedia applications.
- Promote a computer art contest to design new wallpaper art for the library media center computers.
- Give "Bright Idea" awards to faculty and classes who use technology to present subject matter or culminate a curriculum unit. Create a certificate, such as the one in Figure 8.2.
- Hold a Technology Fair at the school. Set up booths in the library media center or another area of the campus. Bring in businesses and parents to demonstrate the technology they use in their workplace or home. Select students to demonstrate their work.
- During morning announcements or the morning broadcast, make a special time for a Web site of the week.
- Create a bulletin board of black paper with white yarn stretched over it to resemble a web. Post Web sites pertaining to the school curriculum on the bulletin board. Call it "(Name of School's) Sightings."
- Use new technology tools to present lessons in research skills. Using a Smart Board with a PowerPoint presentation can peak teacher and student interest in a subject. Younger students become excited when you use the pen to solicit ideas for research.

Conclusion

Successfully engineering a technology-enriched curriculum on the campus takes patience. It requires a commitment on the part of the principal, library media specialist, and if present, the technology facilitator. Each works in concert with the others to provide the ability, the application, and the anticipation of presenting tomorrow to students today.

Helpful Web Sites for Library Media Specialists

- Promoting Technology: 13 ways to do it: More great ideas to pique interest <http://www.nctp.com/promoting_technology.html>
- Developing Effective Technology Plans <http://www.nctp.com/john.see.html>
- The Nine Information Literacy Standards for Student Learning <http://www.ala.org/aasl/ip_nine.html>
- The School Library 101 sponsored by the Three Rivers Regional Library System, Colorado <http://www.colosys.net/three/101/school/index.html>

Chapter 9

Guidelines for Positive Student Behavior

The first step toward a positive library media center environment is to maintain disciplined behavior among the student patrons. The library media specialist must determine the rules of acceptable behavior. After that, the consequences of compliance and infractions also must be identified. The librarian must be familiar with the school district's policy on discipline procedures. This policy is usually available in print form or on the school district's Web site. Some schools include the discipline policy in student handbooks. Be familiar with classroom discipline techniques. For example, some teachers use different colored clips to designate misbehavior. Some schools have a uniform discipline technique and attention commands for school-wide consistency. Check to see if consequences can be enforced in the library.

Starting Out Right

Greet the students each time they enter the library. Create a caring atmosphere in the library media center by learning the students' names as quickly as possible. Conduct students to the area of instruction or storytime. During browsing time, walk around the library and offer assistance. Never allow students to enter an area where they cannot be seen. This protects the student and prevents problems with liability (which, of course, are rooted in the same goal).

Ask the students to contribute to library rules that will enable the library media center to run smoothly. Discuss the consequences of misbehavior with them. Review the contributions from the classes. Revise the mission statement from the various suggestions with the students. Develop library media center rules that are clear and enforceable from the students' suggestions. Now, the rules are more personal, and students' peers approve the consequences. The more students contribute and create, the more they are apt to remember the goals of the library and how they will be attained.

Verbal Cues

Develop methods for gaining student attention quickly. The following verbal methods work well with students in the primary grades. It uses a simple acronym, the letters A-B-C:

A-B-C by Laurie Thelen

All hands in laps (*hands folded in lap*).

Be still as can be (*legs and feet are still*).

Catch the words with your ears.

Let your eyes truly see (*open eyes and attentive face*).

When the students are familiar with this method, simply say the letters A-B-C, and the students are ready for instruction. Practice the letters and action until the students respond.

When one method becomes stale, use another method. One of my favorites is "May I see all of your eyeballs?" Give the students a bug-like stare until all have joined in. When releasing students by groups, play an "I Spy" game. For example: "I spy a table with voices off and books closed." This group becomes the first to join their teacher. Dismiss students by the type of book they checked out. This teaches genre from an early start. "If you checked out a mystery, please join your class" is a sample statement.

Nonverbal Cues

Create an array of nonverbal cues. Classroom teachers have many ways of commanding their students' attention. These cues range from ringing a bell to elaborate hand-clapping techniques. A completely quiet library media center is antiquated and not necessary. Today, students share books with friends, emergent readers need to read out loud, and student projects require people with vocal ideas. Sometimes, it is necessary to lower voice levels out of consideration for others. To quietly cue students to noise level, use a hand signal. Hold your hand with thumb down. Position your fingers up, together and slightly curved, as if measuring a large amount; in this case it is the noise level in the library media center. Then, bring your fingers down to meet your thumb to signal voices to a lower level. If the library media center staff must yell to command attention, something is not right. Preferably, the classroom teacher is present the entire time his or her class is in the library media center. The library media specialist sees hundreds of students each week, so dealing with unfamiliar students and their behavior problems is difficult, especially when one is alone. The classroom teacher can assist in maintaining order, as well as stopping negative behavior before it begins.

Defiant Behavior

Catch disruptive behavior early. The first few moments after an overt, defiant incident are crucial. Do not let the student's misbehavior be the focus of everyone's attention. The verbal communication with the student must be appropriate and inconspicuous. Place the emphasis upon what behavior is expected by using the first person, such as "I (expect, want) you to _____ ." Place the correct behavior in the blank. From my experience, using "I need you to stop _____ " and emphasizing the negative behavior only leads to further confrontation and denial from the student. "I didn't do anything!" is the usual response. Then, the rest of the time is spent in a battle over whether the student did misbehave. Suddenly, the wrong person is controlling the situation, escalating the disruption. In the end, proper behavior (positive) is the desired outcome rather than convincing someone of an infraction (negative).

When students consistently disrupt others in the library or challenge the library media specialist, seek outside help. In some cases, the principal, classroom teacher, student, and the library media specialist devise a contingency contract. This contract defines acceptable behavior and consequences for both negative and positive behavior. Forbidding a student from checking out materials or banishment from the library media center are unacceptable consequences for an elementary school student. Finding ways to address the behavior itself, rather than penalizing library privileges, is the desire. The library media specialist checks off when the appropriate behavior has occurred in the library. If not, the student receives a minus mark, and a consequence occurs. Always record in writing what happened, when it occurred, who was involved, what you did, and who witnessed the incident. When the student corrects his or her behavior, recognize and reward (per the contract) such a success.

Instruction Techniques for Large Groups

In whole group instruction, the students' attention should first be commanded and received. Do not begin your instruction while the students are talking. Focus on the students, and pause until all talking has ceased. Shouting over student talking conveys a negative message loud and clear: inattention is acceptable. It becomes a competition between the library media specialist and a flock of students on a decibel attainment level (no contest!). Maintain a normal tone of voice to prevent confrontation possibilities. Be prepared to overlook minor offenses. Ignoring minor behavior problems helps to extinguish the behavior.

Be enthusiastic about the subject of instruction. Students can tell by voice tone the library media specialist's attitude toward the topic of instruction. Tell students the objectives while the class is in the library media center. Determine time limits for the various tasks, and inform the students at the beginning of the instruction.

Wander about the library, making eye contact with the students. When conducting detailed group instruction, see that all students are with you on each step. If students appear to have difficulty understanding directions or tasks, quietly provide personal attention.

When asking questions, occasionally choose the students who are seated in the back, or simply do not allow any of the students to raise their hands. This ensures student engagement across the research area. The students do not know who will be called to respond, so all are attentive. When speaking, walk around the students' tables to focus attention on the topic. Use the student's name when asking questions. Cueing the students to your instructions creates alertness. Ask open-ended questions, such as "How can I find the information that I need?" Let the students find their way to the answers. When a student thinks critically, the material imprints itself quickly upon the mind.

Keeping Research Skills from Becoming Boring

Employ a variety of teaching methods and media to communicate a learning objective. Some new presentation technologies can add fresh pizzazz to hold attention. For example, the Smart Board is a projection screen with wired feedback to its computer that allows the presenter to interact with the projection. While the Smart Board projects the lesson content, the librarian can ask for student input and students can use the pen feature to write their ideas into the projected content. This eye-catching feature captivates student attention and involvement in the lesson. Use the writing pen as a reward for well-behaved students. All methods become commonplace, so providing a variety of delivery methods is important. Full body activities can perk up student attention. For example, create a cheer for a simple bibliographic lesson to cite sources. An acronym for the parts of a book bibliography lends itself well to a cheer. For example:

A. Author
B. Book Title
C. City: Company
D. Date
E. Every page I used

Hold up cards at the end of the research session with the letters that begin each item. Say, "Give me an A!" The students respond, "A!" Next, yell, "What does it stand for?" Students return with the full word or words the letter represents. Tell the students this is probably the only time they can yell in the library media center, so have fun.

The "Heart" of the School

The library media specialist is often called upon to become a book detective. Sometimes students ask for a book and do not remember the title, the author, or where the book can be found in the library. They just remember their friend said it was great. Gently and tactfully aid the student in its location. If the library media center staff reacts with a negative attitude that communicates "This is a waste of my valuable time," many negative feelings are imparted to the student. Supporting the students' self-esteem creates a lasting impression. The mission of the staff of the library media center is to convey a helpful, caring attitude at all times and truly be the "heart" of the elementary school and the learning community.

Chapter 10

Finding and Keeping Volunteers and Media Clerks

School library media centers are facing a staffing crisis. Many school districts are eliminating funding for paid library assistants, as well as certified librarians. The obvious recourse for the library media specialist is to rely more on volunteer help. However, the traditional volunteer—the stay-at-home parent—has virtually disappeared. Finding library volunteers today is like pulling a rabbit from a hat. Today's library media specialist needs to be a real magician.

Some schools have student populations well over 500, who check out two or more books a week. Multiply these numbers by the time it takes to shelve books and, as a result, the library media specialist is often unable to meet the students' needs for research and literature. As if the daily challenge of re-shelving books were not enough, how does the library media specialist find volunteers to staff special events, such as a Book Fair? In addition, special projects, such as designing and maintaining an award system for reading programs, become almost impossible to manage without some assistance. The school may have poorly attended or nonexistent parent-teacher organizations, so traditional recruitment avenues do not exist.

Therefore, it is time to get creative! This chapter offers suggestions for a successful volunteer program in a school setting. Recruitment strategies, training programs, and volunteer motivation and retention will be explored.

Recruitment

Parents

- Send a letter to parents before school starts explaining the library program and its needs, such as the one in Figure 10.1. Include a volunteer application form on the backside of the letter. You can include this in the school's general mailing to parents before the school year begins. Keep the letter brief, and be specific about job descriptions and the time volunteers are needed most.
- Stress that no experience is necessary. Emphasize that working in the library benefits job resumes and helps fill in gaps within employment histories. Homemakers might be interested in gaining work experience in order to return to the job market.
- During new student registration, place a brochure or flier on the table about the library media center's volunteer needs. Use the Volunteer Information Sheet in Figure 10.2. This form serves as the adult volunteer application form.

Figure 10.1: Letter to Parents

Date:

Dear Parents:

I am the library media specialist at _____ . Our library media center is the heart and hub of our school. We have some great ways for you to volunteer in the library. Below is a list of opportunities:

____ Shelving (our biggest need)
____ Circulation—overseeing students as they check in and check out books
____ Reading one-on-one to students
____ Helping with reading program awards
____ Reading to groups of students
____ Displays
____ Book Fairs

Please consider volunteering in one of the most exciting parts of the school building. Our library media center is warm and inviting. Plus, students love to visit it. Exciting things happen in our library—students create puppets, act in plays, learn research skills, and connect with the school's curriculum. All of these activities inspire them to become lifelong readers. Be a part of the action in the library media center.

Yours truly,

(Name)

Figure 10.2: Volunteer Information Sheet

```
• • • • • • • • • • • • • • • • • • • • • • • • • •
:  LIBRARY VOLUNTEER INFO SHEET  :
• • • • • • • • • • • • • • • • • • • • • • • • • •
```

Name _____

E-mail address _____

Child's name _____

Teacher _____   Room _____

Daytime Phone(s)   _____

_____

How would you like to help?
No experience is necessary   •   Training provided

___ **Re-shelve books**
  Monday through Friday – you pick the day that works best for you

  _____
  and the time that best fits your schedule:

  _____
  (between 9am and 3pm)
___ **Organizational work on the Reading Motivation Program**
  (keeping track of awards and points)
___ **Circulation System Volunteer**
  (help students checkout and check in materials)
___ **Library Research Volunteer**
  (research and pull materials for classroom teachers)
___ **Reading Tutor**
  (Assisting with small groups or individuals)
___ **Book Fair:** (check all that apply – we can use you for a few hours here and
there – you are not expected to be here the entire time!)
  ___ Set up (school hours – no young folks, please)
  ___ Help students during class shopping days
  ___ Help with shoppers on Family Night
  ___ Close out and pack up (school hours – no young folks, please)

| A security check will be made with the police department, with your permission: |
| ___ Yes   ___ No |

Send the form to the school or E-mail the librarian at:

_____

Or mail to: *Or call: School and/or library phone number*
Name
School Name
School Address
Zip code

- Ask to be on the agenda of the PTA meeting. Volunteer for PTA committees, and request help for the library. If the school has a special presentation for kindergarten parents, ask to be placed on the agenda to present a special program. Get creative. Use puppets, magic, or even a short video of the previous year's activities to help the parents remember the library media center program. Be sure to include video interviews with student and adult volunteers discussing why they enjoy working in the library.
- Place a list of library volunteer opportunities on a table in the library at the school's Open House Night.
- During the year, place notices in the school newsletter. Ask classroom teachers if they know of any parents who have expressed an interest in volunteering at the school.

Grandparents

Ask the students if their grandparents might be interested in volunteering in the library. Find out which ones live close to the school. Make a note of the ones who are retired, and call them. Ask teachers if their parents are retired and looking for an opportunity for service. Plan a special Grandparents Day party in the library. Students invite grandparents for a special storytime and refreshments. At the end of the storytime, give information about interesting volunteer opportunities.

Other Groups

- Consider other sources of adult volunteers, such as senior citizens' groups, retired teachers' associations, disabled citizens' groups, and local garden clubs.
- Advertise in churches, synagogues, and fellowship newsletters. Many religious organizations have programs where members are matched with volunteer opportunities.
- Try forming a Friends of the School Library Club in the school. These adults become library helpers and assist with fund raising, similar to their counterpart in the public libraries.
- Tap into centralized volunteer agencies in the school's city or town. Many are listed as The Volunteer Center.
- Invite local community leaders and celebrities to an annual Family Night Reading Program or Read-a-Thon. Invite community groups to meet in the library media center after hours. In other words, be a part of the community, and get the message out about the library program and its needs.
- If your city has a university or college, place fliers in the education department.

Take the library media center needs to businesses and civic groups in the area. Contact the public relations department in these groups and businesses for information and advice. Ask if you may make a brief presentation to a group of interested volunteers. Take along administrative staff, teachers, and students. Model good read-along methods with one of the students:

- Choose a book that interests the student and is age-appropriate. Read it beforehand, if possible.
- Watch the student as the book is read. What emotion do you see on the student's face? Is the student interested in the story? If not, stop and find another book of interest.
- Point out the characters or objects in the illustrations as you read the book to the student. Ask the student what he or she sees in the illustration.
- Ask the student to guess what happens next in the story.
- Be dramatic and use a variety of voices while reading the story—it helps the student to focus, plus it is a lot of fun.
- Ask the student to join in repeating any repetitious phrases.
- After reading the book, question the student about how he or she felt about the story. Tie in the story with everyday activities the student might do. Do not quiz the student about facts in the story. Let the time be a quiet reflection. Would the student do the same as the characters in the book? Why or why not?

Leave several application forms, a map to the school, and a map of the interior of the school. A well planned, creative presentation makes the corporate volunteer program unforgettable.

Advertising

Advertise in creative places for adult volunteers. Try advertising in the local paper, on the radio, and on cable TV. Advertise in "shopper" newspapers, such as *The Green Sheet*. Place notices on community bulletin boards in grocery stores and branch libraries. Advertise in the local college newspaper. Post volunteer opportunities on the Internet by using VolunteerMatch <http://www.volunteermatch.org/>. This Web site is managed by ImpactOnline and has made thousands of matches. Register the library media center as a nonprofit organization at this site. Members of the community find a list of volunteer opportunities by simply keying in their zip code.

Students to the Rescue

- Collaborate with the classroom teacher to create the job position of "library helper." (See details following this list.) Figure 10.3 on page 86 is an example of a student resume form.
- Talk to the principal about implementing a school-wide Job Corps or Angel Club. Teachers and staff post jobs they need to be filled in their areas. Students complete an application and briefly interview with the "employer."
- Form a Library Club for older students. At the first meeting, talk about the service opportunities the club offers to students and teachers. Discuss the benefits of volunteering in the library, such as checking out the new materials first, their picture in the yearbook, and an award banquet at the end of the year.
- Create a Pride Patrol. At the end of every storytime, two students, who have listened quietly, are picked to straighten shelves and push in

Figure 10.3: Student Resume Sheet

Resume of _____

Job desired _____

Previous experience, _____
(if any)
_____

Qualifications _____
(include any
awards received) _____

_____

Hobbies or Interests _____

_____

_____

Teacher _____

Room number _____

bookends. Students from kindergarten to fifth grade can participate in this special duty. As a reward, the students can go to the "treasure box" to retrieve a prize.

● Start an Adopt-a-Shelf program. Assign fifth grade students a shelf to keep straight. At the end of a month, give a reward.

● Periodically take photographs of student helpers in action. Place the photographs on a poster board outside the library. Student helpers love this, and it helps recruit new volunteers.

● Make Friday the payday for student helpers. Load a basket or box with pencils, erasers, fast food coupons, bookmarks, sports cards, and so on. Students pick a prize each week.

The Library Helper Job

Inform the upper elementary grade teachers of the library media center's needs. Then, teachers can create job positions and include a "library helper" as a position. The students build a resume that includes why they want the job; their qualifications, such as previous and related experience; character traits they feel they possess for the job, such as being organized and a hard worker; a list of special honors they have received, such as perfect attendance, spelling awards, and University Interscholastic League achievements; and a list of sports or service groups in which they are involved. The resumes are submitted to the library media specialist, who chooses the best-qualified students.

The Training Program

Adult Training

Training should be brief and at the point of need. A formalized training session is difficult to schedule if the library media specialist is without an aide to manage the library. Many adult volunteers are transient, so conducting lengthy training sessions is not an effective use of a library media specialist's valuable time. Most parent volunteers want a quick explanation and demonstration of the duty. To make life easier for everyone, a quick training program follows:

The Training Plan

1. Create a folder for each volunteer that includes the following:
   ● Library media center handbook (See example in Appendix H.)
   ● List of names of all volunteers in case a substitute is needed (Be sure to include the library's phone number for emergencies.)
   ● Section for notes
2. Go over any important rules and requirements of the job chosen by the volunteer. Emphasize to the volunteer to ask for advice or instruction if they are unsure of anything. Reassure the new volunteer that many questions are to be expected and it is not an inconvenience for the library media specialist to answer them. Help the volunteer feel as comfortable as possible about the new job.

Figure 10.4: Volunteer Checklist Form

Volunteer Orientation and Training Checklist

Directions: Check yes or no to the following statements: YES   NO

I have been introduced to the principal and library staff.   ❏   ❏

I read the Code of Ethics of _____ Elementary   ❏   ❏
     School.

I have been given a tour of the library.   ❏   ❏

I have been shown the location of the volunteer log sheet.   ❏   ❏

I have read the job descriptions and have chosen one   ❏   ❏
     or more I would like to try.

I have been shown how to do the jobs I have selected.   ❏   ❏

I feel competent to do the jobs I have chosen.   ❏   ❏

I would like more training for my job.   ❏   ❏

I would like to change my job.   ❏   ❏

Comments:

_____

_____

_____

_____

_____

Thank you for taking time to fill out this form.

3. Make sure all the equipment needed by the volunteer to complete a task is available before the job is assigned. A little preparation saves not only time, but also embarrassment when materials cannot be located to complete a job. Hang up a clipboard or create a space on a bulletin board for volunteers to post questions or comments.

4. Ask the volunteer to complete the Volunteer Checklist Form (Figure 10.4). This form is helpful to ascertain any areas of training that need to be redone. It also is a useful tool if the volunteer is reluctant to express requests for more training or assistance.

5. Provide a volunteer sign-in sheet even if your school office has one. Keep a log of how many hours each volunteer serves. The log becomes useful at an award banquet and in applying for grants for the school. Many foundations require the total number of hours that volunteers serve and equate a dollar value to this time. This is known as an In Kind contribution on many grant application forms.

Student Training

1. Interview students and rate them according to their experience and ability. The quickest way to do this is to assign a number from one to ten mentally after the interview is completed.

2. Assign one or more of the following jobs:
   - Care for plants
   - Clean tables
   - Help at the Book Fair by keeping items on the tables neat
   - Keep shelves in order
   - Rewind videotapes
   - Search the catalog for teacher materials

3. Make the training session fun for the students assigned as library aides. Set up learning centers with alphabetizing lessons and demonstrations of duties.

4. After training the students on the various tasks, reassert the expectation of quality work. Convey the importance of correctly shelving materials. If an item is incorrectly placed, it cannot be located and will be seen by others as missing. Tell the students to feel free to leave the item on the cart if they are unsure of its location. Set up a cart with a note attached that reads "UNKNOWN."

Volunteer Motivation and Retention

From the moment student or adult volunteers walk through the doors of the library media center, they should feel welcomed and needed. They are important parts of the learning community. The goal is to keep them satisfied with their work in a warm, friendly environment.

Volunteer Center

Try creating a special area for volunteers in your workroom area or some other place in the library. Volunteers can hang coats, handbags, or backpacks there. Keep food on hand. Go to a discount grocery store, and stock up on snacks, such as pretzels. Furnish sodas for aides and volunteers. Buy a mug for each volunteer with his or her name on it, and place it in the workroom. Keep a supply of hairspray, contact lens solution, tissues, liquid soap, and soft paper towels.

Safety Concerns

Never ask a volunteer to do anything dangerous. Volunteers should never handle a student discipline problem. Notify them that they are to refer all such problems to the library media specialist or another person on the staff of the school. Never leave a volunteer alone in the library media center when children are present. Also, be sure to acquaint the volunteer with fire and disaster drill procedures.

Helping Volunteers Feel Special

Make special nametags for each volunteer. Give presents throughout the year, such as stickers, plants, homemade bookmarks, candy, and rubber stamps. Mail a thank-you letter each month to let them know how much they are appreciated. Praise volunteers often and in public. Introduce volunteers to the library staff and the faculty. If the school has an award banquet, present certificates for length of service, for example 25, 50, 75, or 100 hours of service. Schedule these ceremonies twice a year, as most volunteers generally do not serve longer than six months. Publicize these award events in the local paper. Use the radio to thank them publicly, especially during National Volunteer Week, which usually coincides with National Library Week in April. A simple verbal "thanks" at the end of every volunteer's shift is one of the simplest, yet most effective motivators.

Helping Volunteers Feel Important

Provide the adult volunteers with a library card so that they can check out materials for their children and themselves. Purchase books and magazines about parents' issues, and make them available for checkout. Provide more challenging work if volunteers request it. Perhaps they are interested in attending library conferences or shopping with the library media specialist for books for the library media center. Let the more experienced volunteers train new volunteers. Frequently ask volunteers if they are happy with their current job. Reassign them if they feel they are experiencing boredom or burnout. Let them know it is important to you that their experience in the library be pleasant.

Having Fun

Volunteers need to feel they belong to something bigger than themselves. Display photographs of the library media center's volunteers. For students, put the group's picture in the yearbook. Find time after hours to meet adult volunteers socially. Treat the volunteers to lunch on their birthday or other special occasions.

Rewarding Teachers

Thank elementary teachers who send student volunteers to the library media center. Their gift of a volunteer is special—it shows a great deal of thought about the library media center's needs. Reciprocate with tangible and verbal "thank-you's." Remember them with a small gift or card on holidays and birthdays.

Volunteer Evaluation

A standard policy of evaluation of volunteers is an effective tool to ensure quality work. At times, a quick talk with the volunteer is needed. At other times, a more formal evaluation process is appropriate. To ease the tension that a formal evaluation procedure brings, use the Volunteer Self-Evaluation Checklist in Figure 10.5 on page 92. The volunteer and library media specialist separately complete the form and then discuss the results together. The evaluation should reinforce good work qualities as well as point out areas for improvement.

Working with Difficult People

The proper time to correct difficult behavior is early in the relationship with the volunteer. Expectations of performance need to be clearly stated. At the beginning of the volunteer's first shift, review the job requirements. Go over a list of the duties of the job. General library volunteer duties include circulation (checking materials in and out to patrons), copying and placing materials in teachers' boxes, assisting students locate materials, and shelving. Perhaps the new volunteer feels a need to be creative in a particular area. Encourage this, but watch the time spent so that it does not interfere with the jobs that need to be done. Closely monitor the work, and provide feedback. The written list of duties becomes a helpful tool in this process. Expressing disfavor with the parent volunteer is tricky. The process can become a sensitive issue. Sometimes a simple verbal comment, such as, "I sense that you are not happy with your volunteer job in the library," can open up a discussion. Ask if he or she would prefer to work in another position in the library media center or elsewhere in the school. Utilize the Volunteer Self-Evaluation Checklist Form if the volunteer is uncomfortable or does not offer a response. In cases of an abusive volunteer, direct action from the administration is necessary.

How to Afford Rewards

Big dollars do not have to be spent rewarding volunteers. Use fine money or proceeds from a Book Fair to fund items or special events. Many of the following ideas are free or low cost:

Rewards for Students

- Photos in the yearbook or in the hall
- Recognition at special assemblies
- Chocolate!
- Allowing them to check out more books than other students
- Certificates and letters of appreciation

Figure 10.5: Volunteer Self-Evaluation Checklist Form

Volunteer Evaluation Self-Check

Directions: Circle the number that best reflects your feelings about your job.   NA 1 2 3 4 5

NA = Not applicable to my job.
1 = I need more instruction.
5 = I can function without assistance.

I understand the Dewey Decimal Classification System.	NA 1 2 3 4 5
I shelve books with accuracy.	NA 1 2 3 4 5
I read the surrounding shelves for misplaced items.	NA 1 2 3 4 5
I understand the circulation system.	NA 1 2 3 4 5
I can check in and check out students' books.	NA 1 2 3 4 5
I can trouble-shoot when a student has an overdue book or has too many books checked out.	NA 1 2 3 4 5
I know how to issue late or lost book notices.	NA 1 2 3 4 5
I can help students locate materials using the online catalog system.	NA 1 2 3 4 5
I understand how to access other libraries and their resources on the Internet.	NA 1 2 3 4 5

Comments:

_____
_____
_____
_____
_____

Rewards for Adults

- Library cards
- Monthly notes of appreciation
- Simple craft items, such as bookmarks and decorated pots for plants
- Volunteer events: brunch, lunches, shopping trips for new books
- Featuring their picture or a short bio about them in the school newsletter
- Certificates and special awards for those volunteers who help improve your library service

The Media Clerk

Job Description

The media clerk's role is to support the library media specialist in providing an exemplary library media program. At times, the media clerk will wear many hats, such as the following:

- **Office Assistant** The media clerk checks if office supplies, such as tape, staples, pens, pencils, paper, and projector bulbs, are stocked. He or she informs the library media specialist if items are low and need to be ordered. The media clerk assists students in the checkout of materials. Checking in and shelving materials also are part of the job.
- **Program Assistant** The media clerk assists with the maintenance of any reading programs, such as *Accelerated Reader*™, and special fund raisers, such as a birthday book club. He or she informs the librarian of students who achieve recognition status and prepares necessary certificates.
- **Account Assistant** The media clerk records monies received for lost materials, special programs, and fund raisers.
- **Media Assistant** The media clerk assists with the production of a daily broadcast, and locates and assists in the setup of presentation tools, such as overhead projectors, LCD projectors, VCRs, and digital cameras. The media clerk also prepares materials for circulation. This includes printing out labels and barcodes, covering materials, and repairing damaged and worn items. The media clerk assists with inventory and weeding.
- **Education Assistant** The media clerk helps students locate materials. Knowledge of the Dewey Decimal Classification System is required. Familiarity with other search methods is desired.

The Interview Process

Before the interview, take time to personally reflect on the qualities that are most desirable in a media clerk, such as past experience in a library as a media clerk. Office experience also is a key requirement. A team player, a service attitude, and a gentle touch with children are a few of the most important personality requirements. Many hours will be spent with this person, so assessing whether you can work in harmony with him or her is important.

Form an interview committee if one is not in place on the campus. Ask the principal, staff members who are "library focused," and members of the Library Advisory Committee to be present for the interview. Acquaint them with the desirable qualities that are important in a media clerk. Create a list of interview questions, such as the following ones created by librarian Mari Lyn Jones. Give the applicant a copy, and provide a few minutes for a quick review.

Interview Questions

Library and Office Skills

1. What do you think is the role of a media clerk?
2. Describe any previous library experience.
3. What are your expectations about the media clerk job in an elementary school library media center?
4. How do you manage multitasking?
5. Describe a good day in the library. Describe a frustrating day in the library.
6. What type of computer experience and skills do you have?
7. What additional qualities can you bring to the library media program at _____ Elementary School?

Interpersonal Skills

1. Describe any previous work experience with children.
2. How do you interact with children?
3. Describe your responses to the following situations in a library media center:
   Situation One: A library volunteer announces to you that she intends to rearrange part of the library. You are at the circulation desk, and the library media specialist is in the office area.
   Situation Two: You notice the signage needs to be changed on a bookcase while you are shelving books.
   Situation Three: The library media specialist asks you to copy materials while you are shelving books.

After the Interview

Check with the other people on the interview committee about their impressions of the applicant. Listen carefully to any uncertainties and strong opinions. Do not be afraid to clearly express personal thoughts and concerns to the committee. Always check personal references and previous supervisors that the applicant has supplied, even if the applicant is well known by the committee members.

The First Day on the Job

On the first day of the new media clerk's job, go over the list of expected job duties. Create the list on a four by six inch index card, and call it the Expectations List. On one side of the card, list the daily duties of a media clerk. On the other side of the card, list the days when other tasks will be performed. For example, perhaps Friday is the day on which books are repaired. Also, list occasional duties, such as preparing interlibrary loans and filling out receipts for lost materials. The Expectations List also can be a device to redirect the media clerk's service should problems arise. Perhaps the new clerk or volunteer would like to be creative in some area. Help the media clerk to watch the time spent so the day's tasks are completed.

To Do and To Go Boxes

The To Do box contains items or a list of items that need to be accomplished quickly, such as materials requests from teachers, preparation of materials for circulation, receipts to file, and items to be copied.

The To Go box contains overdue notices, items to be mailed, interlibrary loans, materials to place in teachers' boxes, or material holds for teacher and students.

General Information

Use the following guidelines to provide an orientation for the new media clerk:

1. Acquaint the media clerk with the supply cabinet. Labeling helps the new media clerk to find items quickly.
2. Provide the media clerk a copy of the school handbook. Include a list of all teachers and staff members with their job assignments.
3. Explain school policies on absences, discipline, and fire and disaster drills. Each school has a specific plan for exiting the building during a drill. Prepare a map that shows the assistant the route to take.
4. Give the media clerk a school calendar. Note important dates, such as book fairs, special programs, and author or illustrator visits.
5. Familiarize the media clerk with the performance evaluation tools. Make a copy for the media clerk to take home and review. Once he or she is familiar with what is expected, performance is easier to measure.
6. Make sure the media clerk takes the Expectations List and posts it in a spot where he or she can see it readily.

Moments of Joy!

Every library volunteer program should begin with the premise that help is not permanent. Rare indeed is the volunteer or media clerk who returns year after year. If you find that person, move heaven and earth to keep him or her happy. Most volunteers, both student and adult, are there only for a season. Media clerks find better paying jobs. Students in an elementary setting are there at the whim of their teachers. If a special project comes up for their class, they will not be in the library shelving that day. Good student volunteers graduate to middle school and move on. Depending on volunteers is like chasing after the wind at times. The library media center specialist must recruit constantly.

As much work as the volunteer program can be, it does have its moments of joy. Some adults feel useful for the first time in their lives and find it an empowering experience. Other students see their peers helping in the library media center and ask, "Can I be a student volunteer, too?" Then, there is the day when one student helper hands you a drawing of yourself with the misspelled caption at the top: "*The Best Libraryan in the World.*" All of the work and all of the planning seem like time well spent, indeed.

References

Baule, Stephen M. *Facilities Planning for School Library Media and Technology Centers*. Worthington, Ohio: Linworth Publishing, 1999.

Beasley, Meg. Birthday Book Club form. Used by Deep Wood Elementary, 1999.

Berner, Andrew. "The Importance of Time Management in the Small Library." *Special Libraries* Fall 1987: 271–275.

Buzzeo, Toni. *Collaborating to Meet Standards: Teacher/Librarian Partnerships for K–6*. Worthington, Ohio: Linworth Publishing, 2002.

Hauser, Janet. *Help! For Library Media Center Design, Construction & Renovation: A Guide for Consulting*. Oakland Schools, Waterford, Michigan: New Media Information Center, 2001.

Howard, Susan. Personal interview. 10 June 2002.

Information Power: Building Partnerships for Learning. Chicago: American Library Association, 1998.

Jones, Mari Lyn. E-mail to the author. 14 Jan. 2003.

Karges-Bone, Linda. *Grant Writing for Teachers: If You Can Write a Lesson Plan, You Can Write a Grant*. Torrance, California: Good Apple, 1994.

Lance, Keith Curry, Christine Hamilton-Pennell, and Marcia J. Rodney. *The Second Colorado Study: How School Librarians Help Kids Achieve Standards: The Second Colorado Study*. San Jose, California: Hi Willow Publishing, 2000.

Lance, Keith Curry, Lynda Welborn, and Christine Hamilton-Pennell. *The Colorado Study: Impact of School Library Media Centers on Academic Achievement*. San Jose, California: Hi Willow Publishing, 1993.

Texas Education Agency. *Texas Administrative Code, Title 19: Education, Part 2: Texas Education Code, Chapter 61: School Districts, Subchapter CC, Rule 61.1033B.ii.*
<http://www.tea.state.tx.us/technology/libraries/lib_standards_facilities.html>.

Vasquez, Henry. Personal Interview. 5 Apr. 2002.

Witherspoon, Kenneth. "Know Your Needs." Pflugerville ISD Librarian's Meeting. Pflugerville, Texas. 12 Nov. 2001.

Yucht, Alice H., "Mailbox Methodology." *School Library Management Notebook*. Worthington, Ohio: Linworth Publishing, 1998, pp. 14–15.

Appendix A:
Periodicals for Library Media Specialists

Book Links
PO Box 615
Mt. Morris, IL 61054-7564
Phone: 1-888-350-0950
E-mail: blnk@kable.com
Web site: <http://www.ala.org/BookLinks/>

Booklist
PO Box 607
Mt. Morris, IL 61054-7564
Phone: 1-888-350-0949
E-mail: blst@kable.com
Web site: <http://www.ala.org/booklist/>

The Horn Book
The Horn Book, Inc.
56 Roland Street, Suite 200
Boston, MA 02129
Phone: 1-800-325-1170 or (617) 628-0225
Fax: (617) 628-0882
E-mail: info@hbook.com
Web site: <http://www.hbook.com>

LMC (Library Media Connection)
Linworth Publishing, Inc.
480 E. Wilson Bridge Road, Suite L
Worthington, OH 43085
Phone: 1-800-786-5017 or (614) 436-7107
Fax: (614) 436-9490
E-mail: orders@linworthpublishing.com

School Library Journal
PO Box 57559
Boulder, CO 80322-7559
Phone: 1-800-595-1066 or (818) 487-4566
Fax: (818) 487-4550
E-mail: custserv@espcomp.com

School Library Media Activities Monthly
LMS Associates LLC
17 East Henrietta Street
Baltimore, MD 21230-3910
Phone: 1-888-371-0152
Web site: <http://www.crinkles.com>

Teacher Librarian Magazine
PO Box 34069
Dept. 343
Seattle, WA 98124-1069
Phone: (604) 925-0266
Fax: (604) 925-0566
E-mail: subs@teacherlibrarian.com
Web site: <http://www.teacherlibrarian.com>

Appendix B:
Resources to Build Elementary Library Media Center Collections

Children's Catalog. 18th ed. Published by H. W. Wilson. 2001. ISBN 0-8242-1009-3. (An online version is available for purchase at <http://www.hwwilson.com/>.)

Gillespie, John T. *Best Books for Children: Preschool Through Grade 6.* 7th ed. Published by Bowker-Greenwood. 2002. ISBN 0-3133-2068-3.

Homa, Linda L., Ann L. Schreck, and Maureen Hoebener, editors. *The Elementary School Library Collection: A Guide to Books and Other Media.* 22nd ed. Published by Brodart.

Matthew, Kathryn I. and Joy L. Lowe. *Neal-Schuman Guide to Recommended Children's Books and Media for Use with Every Elementary Subject.* Published by Neal-Schuman Publishers. 2001. ISBN 1-55570-431-X. <http://www.neal-schuman.com/>.

McClure, Amy A. and others. *Adventuring with Books: A Booklist for Pre-K–Grade 6.* 13th ed. Published by The National Council of Teachers of English. 2002. ISBN 0-8141-0073-2. <http://bookstore.ncte.org/>.

Tomlinson, Carl M., editor. *Children's Books from Other Countries.* Published by Scarecrow Press, Inc. 1998. ISBN 0-8108-3447-2. <http://www.scarecrowpress.com/>.

Van Orden, Phyllis. *Selecting Books for the Elementary School Library Media Center: A Complete Guide.* Published by Neal-Schuman Publishers. 2000. ISBN 1-55570-368-2. <http://www.neal-schuman.com/>.

York, Sherry. *Picture Books by Latino Writers: A Guide for Librarians, Teachers, Parents and Students.* Published by Linworth Publishing, Inc. 2002. <http://www.linworth.com>.

Appendix C:
Spanish Language, Bilingual, and ESL Publishers

Cinco Punto Press
701 Texas
El Paso, TX 79901
Web site: <http://www.cincopuntos.com/>

Criticas
PO Box 16976
N. Hollywood, CA 91615-6976
Web site:
<http://www.criticasmagazine.com/>
Note: This is a review journal.

Los Andes Publishing Company
PO Box 190
Chino Hills, CA 91709
Phone: (626) 810-6180
Web site: <http://www.losandes.com>

Me+Mi Publishing, Inc.
128 South County Farm Road
Suite E
Wheaton, IL 60187
Phone: 1-888-251-1444
Web site: <http://www.memima.com/>

Multi-Cultural Books and Videos
28880 Southfield Road
Suite 183
Lathrup Village, MI 48076
Phone: 1–800-567-2220
Web site:
<http://www.multiculturalbooksandvideos.com/>

Santillana USA
2105 NW 86th Avenue
Miami, FL 33122
Phone: 1-800-245-8584
Web site: <http://www.santillanausa.com/>

Appendix D:
Directory of Subscription Service Providers

Demco's Periodical Service
DEMCO Periodicals
PO Box 7760
Madison, WI 53707-7760
Phone: 1-800-448-6764
Fax: 1-888-329-4728
Web site: <http://www/demco.com/>

EBSCO Subscription Services
PO Box 1943
Birmingham, AL 35201-1943
Phone: (205) 991-6600
Fax: (205) 995-1518
Web site: <http://www.ebsco.com>

University Subscription Service
Phone: 1-888-USS-1213
Web site: <http://www.ussmag.com/>

Appendix E:
Suggested Periodical Titles for Teachers

Book Links: Connecting Books, Libraries,
and Classrooms
Book Links
PO Box 615
Mt. Morris, IL 61054-7564
Phone: 1-888-350-0950
E-mail: blnk@kable.com
Web site: <http://www.ala.org/BookLinks/>
Note: Published by Booklist Publications

Copycat Magazine
Copycat Press, Inc.
PO Box 081546
Racine, WI 53408-1546
Phone: (262) 634-0146
Fax: (262) 634-0717
E-mail: subscriber_services@copycatpress.com
Web site: <http://www.copycatpress.com>

Instructor Magazine
Phone: 1-800-544-2917
Web site: <http://teacher.scholastic.com/
products/instructor/subscribe.htm>

Mailbox Magazine; *Teacher's Helper*;
Mailbox Bookbag
The Education Center, Inc.
PO Box 9753
Greensboro, NC 27429-0753
Web site: <http://www.theeducationcenter.com>

The Reading Teacher
International Reading Association
800 Barksdale Road
PO Box 8139
Newark, DE 19714-8139
Phone: 1-800-336-7323 or (302) 731-1600
Fax: (302) 731-1057
Web site: <http://www.reading.org>

R T W Magazine (Reading Writing Thinking)
ECS Learning Systems
PO Box 791439
San Antonio, TX 78279-1439
Phone: 1-800-688-3224
Fax: 1-877-688-3226
E-mail: esclearn@gvtc.com
Web site: <http://www.educyberstor.com>
Note: Available in print and online versions

Teaching PreK–8
Phone: 1-800-678-8793
Web site: <http://www.teachingk-8.com>

Appendix F:
Information Literacy Standards

From *Information Power: Building Partnerships for Learning* by American Association of School Librarians and Association for Educational Communications and Technology. Copyright © 1998 American Library Association and Association for Educational Communications and Technology. Reprinted by permission of the American Library Association.

Information Literacy

Standard 1: The student who is information literate accesses information efficiently and effectively.

Standard 2: The student who is information literate evaluates information critically and competently.

Standard 3: The student who is information literate uses information accurately and creatively.

Independent Learning

Standard 4: The student who is an independent learner is information literate and pursues information related to personal interests.

Standard 5: The student who is an independent learner is information literate and appreciates literature and other creative expressions of information.

Standard 6: The student who is an independent learner is information literate and strives for excellence in information seeking and knowledge generation.

Social Responsibility

Standard 7: The student who contributes positively to the learning community and to society is information literate and recognizes the importance of information to a democratic society.

Standard 8: The student who contributes positively to the learning community and to society is information literate and practices ethical behavior in regard to information and information technology.

Standard 9: The student who contributes positively to the learning community and to society is information literate and participates in groups to pursue and generate information.

Appendix G:
Ordering Information for the Colorado Studies

Lance, Keith Curry, Lynda Welborn, and Christine Hamilton-Pennell. *The Colorado Study: Impact of School Library Media Centers on Academic Achievement*. San Jose, California: Hi Willow Publishing, 1993.

Lance, Keith Curry, Christine Hamilton-Pennell, and Marcia J. Rodney. *The Second Colorado Study: How School Librarians Help Kids Achieve Standards: The Second Colorado Study*. San Jose, California: Hi Willow Publishing, 2000.

Order both full reports from Hi Willow Publishing for $25, plus $5 shipping and handling.

Contact: David Loertscher
Hi Willow Publishing
PO Box 720400
San Jose, CA 95172-0400
Phone: 1-800-873-3043
E-mail: sales@lmcsource.com
Web site: <http://www.lmcsource.com>

Appendix H:
Library Volunteer Handbook

Mission of _____ **School Library Media Center**

The mission of _____ School Library Media Center is _____

_____

_____

Code of Ethics

Volunteers are bound by the same code of ethics as teaching staff—to maintain confidentiality regarding each pupil, including progress, behavior, and records. If students tell you of an incident in their lives, please report it as soon as possible to the librarian or someone on the staff.

Punctuality and Attendance

Your attendance and your help are important to the library. Should an emergency arise, please call as soon as possible so other arrangements can be made. Call the school office at _____ or the library media specialist at _____ .

Outline of Duties

Your duties may include some or all of the following:

- Assist with the circulation of materials
- Integrate new materials into the existing collection
- Make simple repairs to damaged materials
- Aid in setting up displays
- Assist students in the location of materials
- Assist in inventories of current materials
- Read with students

Staff of _____ Library

_____ , Library Media Specialist
_____ , Media Clerk

Rules and Regulations for Students Using the Library

_____ Library has only two basic rules:

1. Care for others, including the people who work here.
2. Care for books and library materials.

Should a discipline matter occur, please refer it to the librarian. The school follows a prescribed method of discipline.

How to Help a Student Locate Material

1. _____ Library has an automated catalog in which students can search by author, title, and subject. Words such as "The," "A," and "An" are ignored in title searches.
2. Our library computers also are connected to the Internet as an additional resource for students.
3. Encyclopedias, dictionaries, and atlases are located in the "R" section of the shelves.
4. Magazines are located on a rack in the free reading area.
5. Never tell a student that we do not have information on a given topic. If that appears to be the case, the library media specialist has access to other schools and resources.

The Dewey Decimal System

000–099	General Works	(encyclopedias, reference)
100–199	Philosophy	(ideas about behavior, thought, and psychology)
200–299	Religion	(all religions at all times)
300–399	Social Systems	(education, law, government, customs)
400–499	Language	(dictionaries, grammar)
500–599	Pure Science	(biology, chemistry, physics)
600–699	Technology	(medicine, industry, agriculture, machinery)
700–799	Arts	(music, painting, sculpture, games)
800–899	Literature	(poetry, plays, books about literature)
900–999	History	(history of civilizations, geography)

Floor Plan of the Library (Insert your plan)

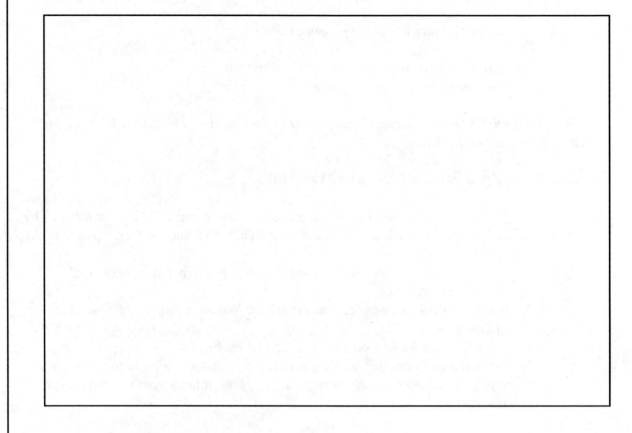

Job Descriptions

Shelver: The job of shelving is important. Without this help daily, many books are not on the shelves when students need them. If you have questions about where to properly shelve a book, please ask the library media specialist. If a book isn't in the right place, students often think it is missing.

Duties:
- Understand the Dewey Decimal Classification System after training
- Check in the books properly
- Correctly shelve books
- Skim the surrounding shelves—check for any misplaced books
- Re-set loose bookends, straighten books that have slipped, keep shelves looking neat and tidy

Reading Program Volunteer: Assists the library media specialist with the management of the reading program

Duties:
- Record the names of students who turn in their reading logs
- Dispense and organize awards

Circulation System Volunteer: Students from second grade to fifth grade are trained to check in and check out their own materials with the hand-held scanner. All of them need supervision to do so. An adult needs to process the kindergarten and first grade student books. Our library does not charge late fees. However, we do charge for lost books.

Duties:
- Be knowledgeable of _____ Circulation System after training period
- Monitor second through fifth grade check in/checkout
- Manually check in and check out kindergarten and first grade books
- Troubleshoot problems with student checkout, such as too many books and overdue books
- Assist with notices to students with late books

Library Research Volunteer:

Duties:
- Use the catalog system to locate materials when teachers need books for curriculum areas
- Collect materials and place them in the teacher's boxes in the mailroom or deliver them to the class

Book Fair Volunteer: The library receives money from book fairs to purchase new materials and provide special programs for our students. Book fairs also are important in the funding of library events, such as author and illustrator visits, educational programs, and storytellers.

Duties:
- Staff the book fair for the evening sales—one night only
- Staff the book fair with adults to monitor losses and maintenance of books
- Staff the book fair with persons for setup and teardown

Thank you for helping us in the library!!

You are a valuable part of our team!

Index

About the Author

Laurie Thelen entered elementary education as a second grade classroom teacher after she earned her degree and certificate from the University of Texas at Austin. Later, she took the opportunity to build a school library for a small private school in Austin. Upon completing MSLIS studies at the University of Texas, she took a position as the first librarian at Copperfield Elementary School in the Pflugerville Independent School District (ISD). Laurie now holds the position of library media specialist for Deep Wood Elementary School in the Round Rock ISD. She lives in Austin with her husband, Bob, where they have raised their two daughters, Jennifer and Haley. In addition to her interest in school librarianship, Laurie holds a Bachelor of Fine Arts degree and enjoys painting in several media, both for personal pleasure and to the benefit of her library and students.